Budap

A Budapest Travel Guide Written By A Local.

The Best Travel Tips By a Local.

Table of Contents

About Our Guides - Why They Are Unique

We were travelers really tired of the typical boring travel guides. When we traveled, we tried to ask friends, or friends of friends who were "locals". That is where we got the best tips by far -- the most valuable ones to enlighten and inform us on our travel destinations.

This guide strives to do the same as the "ask a local", but it is (maybe!) better organized, and more complete. In all our guides, we hire a "local" writer, and then edit to be sure that the guide is complete, unique, fun and interesting. Typically, we won't add maps or photos. You can access all that on the internet and we like to give you only unique and original content that you won't find easily.

Since we use different writers for each city, you will see (after you fall in love with our guides and download more than one), that they are not standardized. Each city is different, each "local" is different, and each guide is different. And we are really passionate about that.

Thanks for being here and we really hope that you like it. Enjoy!

Chapter 1: The City Of Buda And Pest

Hello, or perhaps I should say "Szervusz" (pronounced *ser - voos*) so you can start practicing your Hungarian - because, if you're reading this book, you're probably planning a trip to the pearl of the Danube, Budapest.

I am a born and raised "Budapester" and I plan to share with you my knowledge about this wonderful city. You will get to know some of its best kept secrets and insider tips to ensure you get the most authentic experience out of your trip to the heart of Europe.

Let me tell you why Budapest is a unique travel destination unlike any other European city.

To begin with, Hungary is the quintessential odd country amongst its European sisters. Hungary is smack in the middle of Europe and although it shares a similar history with its neighboring Eastern European countries - being freed from communism in 1989 - it has no language ties to any of its immediate neighbors. Its language is also unrelated to the Indo European family of languages that encompass most European languages. Hungarian is a Uralic language - meaning it originated in the Ural Mountains - and it shares similarities with only two other countries in Europe, which are Finland and Estonia. The Hungarian language also shares many common words with the Uyghur language of Central Asia. The fascinating connection between the two languages, with so many lands and cultures between them, further solidifies the unique, rich background of Hungary.

Budapest is also a land of paradoxes. It is one of the oldest, yet one of the youngest cities in Europe. From the 1st century B.C. to the 5th century A.D. Hungary was part of the Roman Empire, know by the name, Pannonia. The largest settlement of Pannonia was Aquincum, Budapest's oldest ancestor.

The ruins were discovered in the 18th century by a local winemaker. The discovery included: an amphitheater, mosaic floors, tombstones, statues and other artifacts. These items were all determined to date back to the 2nd century A.D. solidifying Budapest as one of the oldest cities in Europe.

However, the story of modern Budapest doesn't begin until 1873. That was when the districts of Obuda (the historic area that includes Aquincum) merged with Buda (the hilly, residential area) and Pest (the then flat, industrialized land). At first they were called Pest-Buda, but I think we can all agree that Budapest rolls much easier off the tongue.

Why should you visit Budapest? If you need any more convincing before we dive into the 'must' dos, sites & eats, let me emphasize the following: Budapest is a vibrant capital that will enchant you with its youthful atmosphere, charm (sometimes overt, other times waiting to be unlocked), pulsating nightlife, and the bonus of abundant thermal baths, unmatched by any other city in Europe.

Budapest has something for everyone. Whether you're traveling with kids, planning an adventurous city break, a romantic escapade, a step back in time or a culinary getaway, look no further. Its character and culture will keep any history aficionado busy exploring every nook and cranny, while its scenic setting overlooking the old Danube will provide the perfect backdrop for that classic album you've been waiting for. Families with kids have a diverse choice in sightseeing and activities for all age groups. The affordable prices of Budapest will only sweeten the deal, so bring the children (and the ones who are children at heart).

Chapter 2: Fun Facts About My City

As a local, I appreciate the city for its "fin-de-siècle" (end of century) European feel. Most of the architecture of the city was built during Budapest's "golden age" that took place around the end of the 1800's. The styles that can be appreciated range from Baroque to Art Nouveau and Neoclassical. Architectural students from all over Europe are encouraged, if not required, to spend time in Budapest specifically to study these modern marvels.

I'm not alone in this sentiment; it is quite apparent that others share my affinity. In 1987, Budapest was added to the UNESCO World Heritage list for the cultural and architectural significance of the Andrassy Avenue, the Banks of the Danube, and the Buda Castle Quarter.

Here are some more fun and interesting facts about my city:

Budapest has been witness to a tumultuous history. The past is present in vantage points throughout the city. Bullet holes from the Second World War and the 1956 Uprising can be still seen on the walls of many older buildings. These stand as quiet reminders of those volatile events.

Budapest has more thermal springs than any other capital. The bathing culture, dating back to Roman times, remains popular today among locals and tourists alike.

You'll also find one of the largest Parliament buildings in all of Europe (dare I say the world) upon your visit to Budapest. This landmark's size is surpassed only by those of Romania and Argentina. Located right on the bank of the Danube, the building is so mammoth, imposing and long, that if you wanted to walk its perimeters it would be equal to about twenty kilometers worth of stairs.

The Danube is over 2,860 kilometers long. The capital cities of Vienna, Bratislava, Belgrade and Budapest can be found along its route.

You will find mainland Europe's second oldest underground metro system here. It opened to great fanfare in 1896, at the time Hungary was celebrating its 1000th anniversary. The M1 (as it is now called) - was inaugurated as The Millennium Underground to mark the celebration. Only London has an older underground in Europe.

The Budapest Zoo is one of the oldest zoos in the world; it opened in 1865. It's frequently listed as one of the best zoos in Europe. CNN recently named it 'the most interesting zoo' in Europe.

Budapest is home to one of the largest music festivals in the world: The Sziget Festival. Every August, 400,000 people converge on Sziget Island (in the northern part of Budapest's section of the Danube) to enjoy a diverse range of musical acts amidst a one-of-a-kind setting.

The second largest synagogue in the world - and the largest in Europe - is found in the heart of Budapest. Built between 1854 and 1859, the Dohany Street Synagogue includes a cemetery, exhibits, guided tours and even musical performances provide a window into Hungary's centuries long Jewish history.

Centuries of Ottoman rule following the Turkish invasion of the 16th century has left an unmistakable mark throughout the city. At one point, most interestingly, Budapest was home to the most northern holy place of Islam. Gul Baba came to Hungary during the aforementioned invasion. After his death in 1541, he was deemed a holy man. Near the Rozsadomb, the small, unassuming chapel where he is buried, has become a sacred place and a site of pilgrimage for the Islamic culture.

Varosliget (City Park) is home to Europe's largest outdoor ice skating rink.

Chapter 3: An Introduction To The City

Budapest can be divided into three areas that are separated by the Danube River. The Danube flows through the heart of the city, with ornate bridges spanning it and connecting the Buda and Pest Banks.

The Bridges of Budapest

At or around the end of World War II, all the bridges crossing the Danube were destroyed. Most have been rebuilt and reopened since.

Although there are several bridges crossing the Danube these main four should be your landmarks, 'must dos' and are part of the UNESCO World Heritage list.

The Chain Bridge (Lanc hid)

The first permanent bridge across the Danube, connecting Buda and Pest was built between 1842 and 1849. It was commissioned by Count Istvan Szechenyi and designed by William Tierney Clark, with the work overseen by Scotsman Adam Clark. It's one of Budapest's most iconic landmarks. The lions decorating the entrances are the work of Janos Marschalko. The opening of the bridge was a sensation in Europe (one could compare it to the opening of the Brooklyn Bridge in New York many decades later). It was rebuilt exactly 100 years after it first opened.

The bridge connects Pest (from in front of the Gresham Palace) to Buda's Clark Adam ter. From there you can take a funicular up to the Castle District. (Note: this funicular is not included in the public transport system unlimited passes).

The Margaret Bridge (Margit hid)

Budapest's second permanent bridge over the river was designed by the French engineer Ernest Gouin. It was first opened in 1876 with an extension completed in 1900. While on the 4,6 tram, you may notice this extension rather abruptly.

This bridge connects Buda and Pest, as well as pedestrians, to Margit Island.

It's one of the best overviews of the city on the Danube.

The Szabadsag (Liberty) Bridge

It connects Pest's Fovam Ter to Buda's Gellert Square. The colors and design help the bridge to blend seamlessly into the architecture on both sides and into the river that it spans. It originally opened in 1896.

The Elizabeth (or Erzebet hid)

Take a detour off Vaci utca to marvel at this bridge, connecting Marcius 15 ter to the northern part of Gellert Hill and the Rudas Baths. The original bridge, a suspension bridge that was ahead of its time, could not be rebuilt after the war. The new bridge was completed in 1964 and its lights were a gift from Japan to Hungary.

Near the Chain Bridge

Go to Raqpart - a great bar and restaurant located on 'not quite a boat' right underneath the bridge. A fun, trendy, affordable place to get a beer and a bite before or after a pleasant jaunt across the bridge. It has excellent views of the river, with boats motoring past you and the castle district right across from you.

On the Buda side is one of my favorite places - the unassuming Lanchid Presszo. The owners are infatuated with classic American rock, but even more so with great local food. Feel free to ask the owner about the rock-and-roll posters plastered on the walls around you. You might just get a great story to go with your great plate of food.

Not far from the Erzebet Hid

Try the Central Kavehaz. Opened in 1887, the cakes and coffee at this cafe are equal to the ambiance and charm. It's traditional but welcoming. And unlike many of the other best cafes you may have a chance to visit; it's open until 23:00. It's a short walk from the bridge but even closer to Ferenciek Ter, which has one of the most impressive views up and down Rakoczi Avenue.

By the Liberty Bridge

Inside the Balna (or 'whale' building), located directly behind the Great Market Hall is Jonas - a great place for beers and snacks. Lots of smiles, great beer and a great view of the bridge and Gellert.

Just a note on the Balna: This is one of the very few structures anywhere, in or even near to the city center, which is obviously not classical or historical at first sight. It wants to be a cultural center with everything from shops and restaurants to art galleries and concert venues (the concert would have to be smallish). Some may comment that the whale-shaped glass dome style exterior of the building does not necessarily fit in with the heritage of its neighborhood - feel free to be your own guide in this case.

Near Margaret Bridge

You cannot beat the pastries at Marodi Cukraszda. If there is a holiday, you may find yourself in line with the residents of district XIII, who take copious amounts of sweets for their celebrations.

Poszonyi Vendeglo may not be the trendiest option near the Margit bridge, but it's the best for local Hungarian food and atmosphere. Being the simpler, less modern option, it can be easily overlooked, but not by those in the know who often pack the place out on evenings and weekends.

Obuda

Obuda is the ancient Roman outpost. It is, historically speaking, the most important district because of the role it played in Budapest's history beginning with the Roman era.

Obuda is the perfect place to acquaint yourself with Hungarian history - you'll be able to explore the well-preserved ruins of the Roman period.

At this site, in 89 A.D., the Acquincum military base was founded by a Roman legion. You can visit the remains of the bath used by the legionaries. The area has been well preserved, with the layout of the original plans marked with English commentaries.

Although a very small site, it is history which connects Hungary to its Western neighbors. From May through

September, Obuda hosts the Aquincum Summer Festival. With careful reconstruction and reenactment, the festival helps you travel back two thousand years and experience the everyday lives of the Romans.

You can travel to Obuda by hopping on the M2 metro line. Get off at Batthyany tér. Take the green HEV to Szentlélek tér. From Szentlélek tér you can access Obuda Island (also known as Hajógyári Island), where the Sziget Festival takes place every summer. During winter, the Main Square in Obuda is home to one of Budapest's many Christmas markets.

Wander around Szentlélek tér and find its few unpretentious cafes and an umbrella themed statue

Buda

Located on the western bank of the Danube, Buda is easily marked by its verdant hills. Buda is the former capital of the Kingdom of Hungary, where you will appropriately find the Buda Castle. The incredible palace complex, built originally in 1265 by King Bela IV, has been in constant change ever since, reflecting the different regimes and historical periods of the country.

Pest

Pest, located on the east side of the Danube, is marked by its lack of unique geographical features. The flat and more business-oriented part of Budapest is home to more attractions for the local and visitor alike. It's here that you'll find The Hungarian Parliament, Heroes Square and Andrassy Avenue.

Dating back to the twelfth century, Pest was an independent city. It was almost entirely destroyed in 1241 during the great Mongol invasion of Hungary. Later, in the 19th century, Pest saw the wrath of the Danube, as it overflowed and flooded a great part of the city. In recent years, severe weather and flooding has become an issue.

The Districts

Budapest is a city of 23 districts. The districts are numbered and mapped in the form of a snail. You'll find that most of the major attractions are in the following districts in Pest: V, VI, VII, and XIII, with a few following in VIII.

In Buda most are in districts I, II and III. Don't feel that you are not getting an authentic experience if you can't visit all the districts. Many are residential, with a mix of simple homes, newer constructions or standard communist style flats typical of former Soviet bloc countries. Wander the backstreets to discover more hidden gems and to mingle with the locals.

Chapter 4: Getting Around Budapest

Getting around the city is fairly easy - due to the river that splits the city in two, the eight different bridges and impossible-to-miss landmarks, such as the Parliament and Buda Castle. These make it possible for even the most novice traveler to orient themselves.

While most of the city is walkable and the center is increasingly becoming ever more pedestrian friendly, Budapest is quite massive. Public transportation is a must. Compared to many other big cities, Budapest's transport system is clean (especially the metro) and user friendly. Get a pass for the duration you are visiting to save money - and don't forget to validate it. Although single tickets are sold, a pass is always the better option. You can choose from many options such as 24 hours, 72 hours, one week and longer. Ticket controllers prey on the naiveté of tourists, so don't give them that satisfaction and save yourself the trouble of paying the fine validating your ticket! (Or again, get an unlimited pass)

The pass enables you to take unlimited rides (within the time period chosen) on all modes of public transport - buses, trolleys, trams, the metro and even the boats (in spring and summer).

The Metro

Compared to many big cities with transit systems, Budapest's metro is very user friendly. It also gives you a glimpse of the city's past, present and future:

Metro 1 - The oldest metro line on continental Europe (London's underground is older). You'll feel like you've stepped back a century when you see the small yellow cars - low headroom, tiled stations with warm, turn-of-the century features in the cozy stations. Use this line to reach the Opera House, Heroes' Square and Varosliget (City Park), Vaci Utca (take the M1 to Vorosmarty Ter; from that square you'll be at the start of this main shopping street). Metro1 runs just below street level and is therefore easy to navigate. Hopping on and off at each of the stops can be quite convenient, even if some of them are close enough to each other to be easily walkable.

Metro 2 - The newer line (it was the newest before line 4 opened in the spring of 2014). This line leaves you directly at The Parliament (stop Kossuth Lajos ter), Keleti Palyaudvar (the name of the metro stop as well as a major train station for connecting Budapest to the rest of Europe), and Batthyany Ter (a great place to get views of the Parliament and to start your 'ascent' to the Castle District for the adventurous). Metro 2 - and Metro4 - are by far quieter and comfortable to ride than Metro 3 and Metro1.

Metro 3 - Want an idea of what it was to travel during communist times? The old Soviet era cars will transport you back to those times with ease. If you can brave the noise, dust, and sometimes crowds, use this line not only to get you where you need to go but to get connected to locals from many districts and walks of life. Take this line to goes to Nyugati Palyaudvar (a major train station that takes you to all points west of Budapest, as well as a few international destinations. West End mall is also here), Lehel Ter (for one of the best markets in Budapest), Nepliget (the domestic and international bus station), Corvin Negyed (a mall, pedestrian area, restaurants, and ruin pubs). Take this line to the last stop (Kobanya Kispest) to connect to the 200E bus line. The 200E will leave you right at the airport.

Metro 4 - Opened only in March of 2014 the new metro is an impressive display of modern industrial design with hints of quirk (Szent Gellert Metro Station is my favorite). Each station has its own unique features to contrast the Star Trek like decor. Take this line to reach Keleti Palyaudvar (Train Station), Kalvin Ter (where the National Museum resides), Fovam Ter (to the Great Market Hall), Szent Gellert (to start your climb up to Gellert Hill and its second to none view - or to the Gellert Baths), and Allee (there is a mall, and a smaller but worthy local market right next to it. It's also a great place to start your wander around leafy district XI).

Trams

There are several trams around the city. Trams are always yellow and run above ground with overhead electric wires. The most important ones for a visitor are the following numbers:

4,6 - They make a wide sweeping semi-circle, beginning and ending in Buda, while crossing most of the major avenues throughout Pest. These trams also have stops at which you can connect to every major metro line. You may want to ride the entire length of either of these trams to get an overview of the heart of the city. If you do, just make sure you get a seat as it can get very crowded, which would simply defeat the purpose of trying to catch sight of what you are passing by.

Even better, get off at the Margit Bridge to get one of the best views of the city. Incidentally, this tram line has the longest tramcar in the world. The busiest stop on this tram line - and indeed all of Budapest - is Blaha Lujza Ter. Many people transfer here to Metro 2 or to the busy bus lines on Rakoczi Avenue.

2 - Better than a sightseeing bus; it takes you to most of the notable places along the riverfront in Pest, helping you to see the notable sights and places across the river in Buda - and maybe discover new ones of your own. Some of the stops on this line can be a little bit hard to locate, but don't let that discourage you. Just explore as you go and enjoy the sights around you. For example at March 15th Square (Marcius 15 Ter), there is a carving in the sidewalk underneath your feet displaying the sites of all the Roman ruins along the length of the Danube in Hungary.

1- A great tram to ride if you want to get to know the

city outside the city center. It has the same semicircle idea going for it that the 4,6 line does, only even bigger. It stops at Nepliget (the main bus station), Puskas Ferenc Stadion (a major concert and sports venue; there is also a major domestic bus station here), goes through a few major business and residential districts, and over Arpad Bridge (the longest bridge in Hungary) heading to Obuda.

47, 49 - Take either one of these trams that run on the same track from its start at Deak Ter (the de facto city center). It's first three stops are all really great places to get to some of the best squares/hubs (Astoria, Kalvin Ter and Fovam Ter) or just get lost in the most charming back streets and hidden gems of Pest. Keep going over the Liberty Bridge (which has great views just like the rest of the bridges) to Gellert or Moricz Zsigmund korter.

Bus

The bus network in Budapest is vast, extensive, and quite convenient. As far as the city center is concerned, here are the buses you should probably know.

Bus 16 and Bus 16A starts at Deak Ter, takes you across the Chain Bridge, and will drop you off at the top of the Castle District. The first stop at the top is closer to the Castle and the President's office; continue to the next stop if you would rather go straight to Matthias Church and Fisherman's Bastion. The hike back down should be quite pleasant, but if your knees aren't up for it, you can take the bus, too.

Bus 9 is a good alternative if you would rather stay above ground then take Metro3. Between Kalvin Ter and Nyugati Train Station, it essentially makes the same stops and is much more scenic, even if it does take a several minutes longer. You can also take this bus to Obuda.

Bus 105 is the scenic aboveground alternative to Metro 1 for the entire length of Andrassy Avenue. It also takes you across the Chain Bridge to Clark Adam Square, which is right at the bottom of the Castle Hill. You can get off there and take a ride on the funicular, which is a very short cog railway ride to the top of the hill. Your transit pass does not cover the funicular fee. If you continue on Bus 105, it will take you through the massive arched tunnel under Castle Hill and onward into Buda.

There is a good chance, that along the length of your trip here, you decide you could use a few moments of relief from the excitement of the city center and a few breaths of fresh air. Perhaps, though, you don't want to spend all day travelling to arrive at some other greener destination in the countryside.

No worries. Your transit pass includes access to locations in the Buda Hills, while still within the city limits - and also offer you what you want in terms of natural refreshment.

For example, here is one suggestion for an afternoon away from the hustle and bustle. Take Metro2 to Szell Kalman Ter (the stop just before its terminus on the Buda side). Transfer here to tram 59 or 61 and head off northwest. Get off at Varosmajor Park. This is the lower terminus of tram 60, which is actually a cogwheel railway - its uphill climb to destination is a twenty minute or so relaxing view of some of the small streets and staircases that wind themselves ever congestion-decreasingly upwards into the Buda Hills.

If you so choose, you can connect to the Children's Railway at the top (also a cogwheel type), on which the conductors are actually children. This line winds its way for a few kilometers through the wooded areas of the Buda Hills. Alternatively, you can simply hike around in the hills and enjoy nature on foot before your descent back into town for dinner.

Let's also recognize Budapest's trolley buses and the role they could play in your enjoyment of this city. Do you have such vehicles where you are from? They run with overhead electrical lines just like so many of the trams here. The difference is that they do not run on tracks; rather, they have rubber wheels like regular buses. Many of the trolley bus routes take you twisting along multiple paths turning down streets that no trams or other buses run down.

For a behind the scenes look at some of the college neighborhood streets near Corvinus and Semmelweis, take trolley bus 83 from Harminckettesek (32nd) Tere (where you can connect to tram 4 and 6) to its final stop at Fovam Ter, in front of the Central Market Hall.

Chapter 5: Cruising the Danube

The Danube is the second largest river in Europe. It originates in the Black Forest of Germany and courses through ten different countries, finally spilling into the Romanian coast of the Black Sea. The Danube maintains an important role in the preservation of nature, commerce and infrastructure in the countries it flows through.

Budapest is the largest city settled around the Danube and, as you can imagine, it's the lifeline of the city. One of the most authentic experiences you can have while visiting our capital is a cruise on the Danube. If you can take a boat during the evening when all the bridges and buildings along its banks are illuminated, it can make for a very romantic, enchanting atmosphere. It isn't a rare sight to see someone propose on the deck while travelling down the lyrical river.

You can cruise on the Danube for free - or close to it. How? If you purchase one of the Budapest metro passes: the public transport boats are included on weekdays (simply show your ticket to the boat captain). This does not apply to single ticket holders. On weekends, the pass is not valid on the boats.

When walking along the promenade, on the Pest side, look for D11, D12, D13. The boats indicate whether they are traveling north or southbound. The boats are very slow, as they make frequent stops. But the pace and the view make it one of the most economical and pleasant ways to see the city.

Depending on the water level, sometimes the boats can't stop everywhere. Many of the stops are an easy walk from a tram or metro station.

If you happen to travel to Budapest during the designated month of European vacations (during August), then you should know that on the 20th of August we celebrate an important national Holiday -

Stephen's Day. Do as the locals and take a boat tour to watch the fireworks as they dazzle and add to the breathtaking views of the city. All the while you are relishing in authentic Hungarian cuisine and listening to majestic Hungarian orchestra music. If this holiday falls on a weekday, remember shops and shopping malls are closed, so plan ahead!

Cruises take place all year round. You may not have the fireworks, however, the twinkling lights of the buildings along the Danube will provide the entire light spectacle you need for a night to remember.

There are many boat tours and cruises available for your enjoyment. Every day at approximately 19:00 many tour companies offer an evening cruise with dinner and live music. You can enjoy a four course dinner, drinks and a priceless night vista of Budapest. This is one the best ways to experience the magnificence of Budapest.

During the day - and for less than half the price - there are wine tasting sightseeing cruises. The duration is about one hour and 45 minutes. You'll have a 'tour' of Hungarian wine culture against the backdrop of spectacular views.

Look for the following tour companies - Legenda, Silverline and Budapest Danube Cruise

Chapter 6: See Budapest Through A Local's Eye

Experiencing Budapest through a local's eye is the best way to find out about the hidden gems of the city. The touristy spots and the well known attractions are not to be missed either, but stick around and I'll tell you which are the best thermal baths or where you can find a wallet friendly eatery and mingle with Budapesters.

The most important place to socialize in the life of a resident of Budapest is the one-of-a-kind thermal bath.

A guide to the Thermal Baths

Sitting on approximately 125 thermal springs, Budapest is also referred to as the "city of healing waters". The number of spas, thermal baths and pools make "taking the waters" the norm if you are a local, a custom that dates back to Roman times. Whether you are looking for its therapeutic benefits, for recreation, or both - you will certainly have your pick. The baths originate from three different time periods. There are three main main styles of thermal baths:

The Turkish Baths (Veli Bej, Rudas and Király), which date back to the 16th century Ottoman occupation

The ones built in the **Art Nouveau** style of the 20th century during the golden age of Budapest (Gellért, Széchenyi and Lukács Baths).

The new modern "spas" popping all over the town. (Oxygen)

So, tell me what kind of person you are and I'll tell you which thermal bath to go to.

Most of the Budapest baths have a similar layout, hosting a series of indoor thermal pools, steam rooms, cold plunge pools and areas for massage. Due to the high temperature of the water, many baths are open to guests year round, while the ones that have outdoor pools will be open during the summer/warmer months. Makes sense, right? Just make sure you check the schedule of each one before your visit, because baths can be for men or women only. Széchenyi is always open for both men and women, so the use of swimming suits is mandatory; therefore, don't forget to bring yours, unless you really want to rent one.

Turkish Baths

You will find four baths built during the 150 years of Ottoman Occupation circa the 16th and 17th century.

Király is one of the oldest baths in town, standing for an incredible lapse of 450 years. Arszlan Pasha commissioned the bath after conquering Buda in 1565. The octagonal roof of the original Turkish bath can be spotted from outside.

In the 18th century public bathhouses were added to the original Turkish construction because most apartments in the city weren't equipped with indoor plumbing - this facilitated residents of Buda to bathe in the public bathhouses. The hot water of the bath is rich in minerals, making it very beneficial in treating joints, arthritis, or spinal problems.

Rudas Bath is one of the most famous of the Turkish baths; and its octagonal pool flanked by the high arches makes it very appealing and appreciated by both locals and tourists. The bath was originally built in 1550 and it was recently renovated and improved with more pools, including a Jacuzzi that offers panoramic views of the city.

Until 2006 this bath was traditionally men only, but now it is open to women on set days and on weekends both men and women are allowed. Rudas has a special night program with hours from 20:00 - 04:00. It's hard to imagine another place where one can relax in a hot spring, located in a historic district, in the middle of the night admiring one of the world's most beautiful cities.

Veli Bej is one of the oldest and most famous baths in Europe. Recently refurbished, it combines its old style charm with modern day facilities. The bath has five thermal pools rich in minerals. There is also a swimming pool and saunas. It's important to note it closes for three hours in the middle of the day. It can also be hard to find: it's located next to the larger Lukas baths in Buda, near the Margit Bridge. My personal favorite, its ambiance and quiet are ideal for those of us who want to soothe our body and mind

The Art Nouveau Baths

There are several baths that were built at the turn of the 19th-20th century and the architecture alone is worth paying them a visit. After walking around the city and going up and down the steep streets of Buda

Hills, these places will literally be an oasis of relaxation with an added bonus of healing powers.

The beautiful and elegant Art Nouveau Gellert Bath is now open to both men and women at all times and it has some of the most beautiful indoor swimming pools in the entire city, with clear waters surrounded by ceramic tiles, high Roman style columns supporting a glass roof.

The outdoor swimming pools have a wave machine, making it the best option for travelers with kids - it's a great activity for the whole family. Since it is so popular among tourists and locals, keep in mind it's one of the priciest baths in the city.

Széchenyi Bath is a huge bath complex located in the largest park in Budapest, Városliget. You can read all about Városliget in the chapter "Budapest's Natural Treasure" so make a day of it and enjoy all the other attractions found in the park, including the zoo. The bath complex is open year round, having both indoor and outdoor pools.

Széchenyi Bath (like many of the others, notably Gellert and Lukas) provides all sorts of therapeutic treatments. There is even a restaurant inside if you get hit with a voracious appetite after all the water fun. A fun endeavor locals picked up from years of going to the baths is playing chess on floating boards as they soak. It's exciting, busy, and a highlight to many people who visit.

Lukács Baths is the first bathhouse in Budapest, opened around the 12th century to provide healing waters to the knights occupying the city. It was then rebuilt at the turn of the 20th century. Lukács Baths is not as popular among tourists as the previous two, so if you are looking to experience the bath like the locals, this is the perfect choice. Here you will find outdoor and indoor pools and baths, saunas, Turkish hammam and a sun terrace.

Make sure to bring your own towel, bathing suit, and shoes suitable for water. Most of these baths have lockers to rent. Renting suits and towels, has an additional cost. When arriving, you may be a bit overwhelmed. Take a breath, be patient, walk around the facilities - get your bearings. It's worth it!

Important Historical And Cultural Sites

What I like about Budapest is that it is extremely walkable and accessible by public transportation.

Most of the cultural and historic sights to be crossed off your list can be reached by taking tram number 2. It's one of the most scenic transportation routes in the world. Running along the Danube on the Pest Side you can take it to the Museum Palace of the Arts, one of Budapest's newest and largest musical venues. Get off right at Fovam Ter, where you'll find the Great Market Hall; or Vigado Terrace -a recently renovated historic building, great place to watch performances - to explore the Parliament building. The tram's northern terminal is at Jaszai Mari Ter, where you can access Margaret Island.

While on the tram across the Danube, you'll be able to see Gellert Hill, Buda Castle, Fisherman's Bastion, Varkert Bazar, Rudas Baths and Batthyany ter.

Buda Castle Hill or Castle District is one the oldest areas of Budapest, dating back to the Middle Ages. Due to the importance it played in Budapest's development, this area has been marked as a World Heritage site. The Castle District includes the Royal Palace, Matthias Church and Fisherman's Bastion. The area has no shortage of historical monuments, making it ideal for a walking tour any time of day, but especially in time to catch the panoramic view from Fisherman's Bastion as the sun sets behind you. Take note of the roofs in the area with many patterns reflecting the Turkish influence of the area. Stay for the evening and enjoy dinner in one of the district's intimate restaurants.

St. Stephen's Basilica is impressively grand, placed second after the Hungarian Parliament in largest monuments in Budapest. The church is named after Hungary's first king, Stephen (975–1038) and it's said that his right hand is buried in the reliquary. The southern tower also holds the record for Hungary's biggest bell.

The church also plays a role of great importance in the music scene of Budapest. If you are lucky to catch a classical concert during your visit, don't miss the amazing organ performances. For a few Euros, you can go to the top for a different perspective of the city.

It's impossible to talk about Budapest and not mention its famous bridges over the Danube. The Chain Bridge is the most well known bridge and is also a symbol of Budapest, as it was the first permanent stone bridge; and, following its construction, the cities of Pest and Buda were united in the mid 19th century. At the time of its construction it was regarded as one of the most modern engineering wonders. A walk across the bridge is a must for any traveller.

Another World Heritage Site is the Danube Promenade, running along the length of the Danube on the Pest Side. Start at Petofi Bridge and keep going all the way to Szent Istvan Park - a bit past the Margit Bridge. The promenade is the perfect way to sightsee all the attractions that are located on the banks.

Don't miss the Shoes on the Danube Memorial, an incredible piece of performance sculpture that honors a sad episode in Hungary's long history of tragedy. The memorial was conceived by film director Can Togay in collaboration with sculptor Gyula Pauer to bring honor to the victims of the Fascist militiamen of Arrow Cross during World War II. As the sculpture indicates, the Jewish people were ordered to take off their shoes on the edge of the water - then they were shot into the river. The sculpture shows the shoes that were left behind on the bank.

The Parliament Building is probably the most striking monument in a city with so much beauty. Even locals can't help but wander in front and around it. On the Buda side, especially at night, the beautiful illumination compliments its architecture. The structure was built to celebrate the Hungarian Millennium in 1896 and now it houses the Hungarian Crown, used by King Stephen. Its interiors can be visited on tours if you simply walk down the stairs to the left, then go through airport-like security and pay a considerable fee.

If you're a fan of Art Nouveau, you will love the Gresham Palace, a superb rendition of the city's finest Art Nouveau architecture with restored mosaics and stained glass. It has been turned into a Four Seasons Hotel, possibly the most expensive hotel in town. You can explore the lobby at no cost and have an exorbitantly priced cup of tea in its wonderful restaurant.

Markets

Central Market Hall

Located on the Pest side, about a block away from Liberty Bridge - which is just south of the Chain Bridge - the Central Market Hall (or Great Market Hall) is the biggest food market in all of Budapest.

Since its renovation, it has been attracting many tourists, but residents continue to do their shopping here, picking up vegetables, fruits, specialty foods, fish and meats. The Central Market Hall, resembling an old train station, is a bustling and cavernous edifice consisting of three floors.

Each of the floors has a variety of souvenir shops. The first floor, at street level, is where fresh produce, baked goods, meat, and spirits are sold. At the back end of this level, you'll find an excellent cheese section. Souvenirs on this floor consist mostly of gift-packaged paprikas and other agricultural specialties. In the more crowded, narrower upstairs, you'll find a dizzying array of handicrafts, leather goods, and more upscale souvenirs. There is an area with numerous food stalls where you can try our most beloved dishes, such as langos, wine, and beer. Be ready to browse the area before settling on a souvenir, because prices can drastically differ from merchant to merchant.

In the basement level, there is fish (you won't deny it as you walk downstairs and smell it) and pickled produce, a few souvenir shops with some crafted wooden spoons and affordable postcards, and an Aldi - a good budget grocery store.

The Central Market Hall should be the perfect place for you to get those Hungarian gifts everybody is waiting for back home.

TIP: To learn more about Hungarian cuisine, try one of the cooking classes offered in the Market, available in English as well. They usually include a guided tour of the Market.

Lehel Market

As you approach Lehel Market on the street, the sight of the building may make you think of a fun-house style (albeit lackluster) replica of a cruise ship. Its exterior is hard-pressed to be more misleading. Indoors, you will find a market floor filled with dozens of fresh produce stalls, surrounded by meat, cheese, bread, and pickle shops. There are also several variety/snack stores along the street side of the building. On the upper level, there is a section of clothing and accessory stalls, convenience shops, a handful of small eateries and drinking booths, and a post office. In one of the far corners you will also spot a unique display of mushrooms, identifying many edible and non-edible types (incidentally, the Central Market Hall has a similar display in the back of the main level).

Lehel Market is far less frequented by tourist groups - it really is all about locals stocking up on fresh produce. That is what makes it such a worthy destination - you get a good slice of real Budapest. Plus, if you plan on cooking for yourself, the produce is as good as you can find in the city center.

Belvarosi Market

Not far from the Parliament and even closer to the U.S. Embassy, this market is a great place to mingle with locals, diplomats, and businessmen. Bright, airy and clean, the ground floor has vendors selling everything from seafood, artisan cheese to local honey. There are also coffee stalls and a fresh juice vendor. The food stalls are more specialty and high end, but definitely worth a look. Upstairs you will find one of the best food courts in Budapest.

Rakoczi Ter Market

Rakoczi Ter Market is in a very-easy-to-reach location, at the same named metro stop. It is a worthy stop if you want to shop or just add to your architectural photo collection. The building seems to be a small cousin to the Central Market Hall (minus the second level of souvenirs). There are a couple of very traditional langos and lunch stalls in off to one side. If you are into cheese, check out one stall that sells feta made from four different animals such as buffalo, cow, goat, and sheep. One corner of the market floor has a bring-your-own bottle wine filling station. There are six or eight barrels to choose from. They also sell bottles, if you don't have your own empties.

The northwest corner of the building has one of the best Asian/Chinese markets in the city center. It's a great way to introduce yourself to the grittier, but open eighth district.

Hunyadi Ter Market

The Market at Hunyadi Ter is much less assuming size-wise than Central Market Hall or Lehel Market; its advantage is that it is not on a main street, so there is rarely a crowd to push through. It is more straightforward, so you won't be overwhelmed with choices. But that doesn't mean there is nothing interesting to find. One of the dairy stalls sells fresh sheep's milk, among other things.

Also, the Market is just across the street from one of the nicest small parks in the city center. The park is dog-free, has a section of exercise apparatus, and has a fountain surrounded by benches at its center. The street side facing the Market building has a line of awnings during better weather that sports a street market, expanding the indoor market with more fresh produce, fresh flowers, etc.

Fény Utca Market Hall

Buda's answer to Pest's Great Market Hall, this market is located behind the Mammut Mall at Lovohaz utca 12. Thousands come here daily for produce, dairy, meat fish, plants, pastries, local dishes and handmade goods. It's not a tourist destination - more reasons to go there first.

Jewish Budapest

It is believed the first Jews settled in Budapest at the request of King Bela IV, who moved the Royal Seat to Budapest and invited Jews to populate the new town in an effort to increase its population. When Budapest was formed in 1873, the documents indicate it had a population of 45,000 Jews; however, by 1930 their population increased dramatically to over 200,000.

The Jewish Quarter is located in the City Center and, even though the area is in a state of constant change with new shiny apartment complexes rising up next to the crumbling facades, it is still a charming area to wander into for a peek into Pest's once blossoming Jewish life. You can spot the names of Jewish stores now fading away or the menorahs on displays in the balconies. In the Jewish Quarter, you will find the largest synagogue in Europe, the Dohány Street Synagogue. In the surrounding area you will find numerous monuments attesting to the historical influence of the Jewish heritage in the city's development.

Look for the Jewish Museum, Heroes' Temple, and the Jewish Cemetery.

District XIII's Raoul Wallenberg Utca honors the Swedish diplomat who saved tens of thousands of Hungarian Jews at the height of World War II.

BONUS TIP

One of my favorite places in Budapest is also one of the most unique museums I have ever encountered: the Pinball Museum. If you are travelling with kids (or if you are still a kid) this is the perfect location to spend a couple of hours, especially if it's too hot or too rainy to walk around. The museum is home to a huge collection of vintage pinball and arcade machines that you can still play with!!! There are over 100 pinball machines starting from the 1920's and running up to the present day, all in perfect working condition, and you don't have to pump them full of coins like at a normal arcade. The admission fee grants you free access to all these wonderful machines. The museum has only been open since April 2014 and quickly managed to put itself on the list of the hottest attractions in Budapest, mainly because of the owner's passion. It's open Wednesday through Sunday, from four until midnight! Opt for the supporters ticket for unlimited play and a personal tour.

Museums

In addition to the museum-like markets and baths that we have discussed above, Budapest also holds many real museums within its center (for example, the Pinball Museum - see my Bonus Tip above). Here is a breakdown of just a few of the highlights, in no particular order. I am not telling you what to do; surely you can find something you will like. Please do notice though, I have tried to include some suggestions for side trips in the surrounding neighborhoods once you are at each museum.

Hungarian National Museum

The largest museum in Hungary is the Hungarian National Museum, located on Museum Korut, just a few paces away from the Metro 3 stop at Kalvin Ter. If you are a history buff and want to learn more about Hungary's history, this is the one you should come to.

On the other hand, if you just want to glance around, the building itself and the grounds surrounding it are nice and quiet. You can also continue strolling northward up Museum Korut towards Astoria. If you cross the street to the west side, just before you get to McDonald's at Astoria, there is a covered passageway (Museum Korut 7) leading to the parallel street behind (Magyar Utca). As you walk through, you will notice that the cobblestones under your feet are not actually stones - they are wooden.

There are several shops to browse in this udvar (courtyard): a bookstore, and a little coffee shop. Pass through to Magyar Utca (which translates as Hungarian Street) and take a left. On the next block is a relaxing little park (called Karolyi Kert). You can sit for a few minutes and then continue on westward. At that point you are only a couple of minutes walk from Karolyi Utca, which is stuffed with shops and restaurants.

Also, near the Hungarian National Museum is one of my favorites streets in Budapest - Krudy Gyula utca: about three blocks of some of the best varied restaurants and shops in the area. Everything from a cafe packed with students (Zappa) and all organic grocery store, multi level restaurant (Darshan) and vintage goods shop - it's yet another expression of a city with something for everyone.

House of Terror Museum

Located at Andrassy Avenue 60, the Museum known as the House of Terror occupies a building on the corner of Csengery Utca that would otherwise just blend into the background. It would be too easy to miss the place, even though it is steeped in notoriety. For easy identification, though, the building has been wrapped with an edifice that displays the word TERROR along its western and southern facades - and a star and a cross, right on the corner.

Given the modern undue sick fascination with the macabre and the saturation of horror-related themes in pop-culture entertainment, it is understandable that the sign might cause the naive to assume it actually serves the purpose of entertainment along those lines (or a celebration of those things). I am not sure if my thoughts would lead the designers of the sign to rethink their work, but hopefully it is informative and clears things for those of you who actually want to look a little deeper into the world around you and understand its past.

The House of Terror was the headquarters for the secret police during communist times, where interrogation and torture took place. The Museum is now an exhibition of what happened in the last century in connection with the Nazis and the Soviets, as well as the Hungarian Fascist Party.

If you need a place to reflect after your visit here, or need some refreshment afterwards, just continue on Csengery Utca. Crossing Andrassy Avenue will bring you to Hunyadi Park.

Please refer to the sections about Hunyadi Market and Hopfanatic Pub for more information about this little area.

Castle Museum/Hungarian National Gallery

I have already mentioned Buda Castle and its significance as a landmark and tourist attraction in its own right, but now let's take note of the two museums that the building itself actually houses. They are the Budapest History Museum (or we can just say Castle Museum) and the Hungarian National Gallery.

In case you didn't get enough history from the Hungarian National Museum, you can supplement it here. The National Gallery has several exhibitions that highlight the very best of contemporary and classic art as it pertains to the history of Hungary.

Chapter 7: The City of Music

Budapest is a cultural hub for any art form; however, music especially resonates throughout the city and throughout Hungary's history as one of the city's most prominent exports. Hungarian composers and musicians are famous in the world and have reached the four corners of the earth, playing for world-famous orchestras. That may be due to the excellent musical education that can be found in Budapest. The first Academy of Music was established in the 19th century, where Franz Liszt educated his students.

Nowadays modern music is just as prevalent as classical music here, with the Sziget Festival bringing half a million music enthusiasts every summer to the Hungarian capital.

Classical Music Concerts

The old Liszt Ferenc Academy of Music has been refurbished and it boasts impressive architecture, turning it into the perfect place to attend a famous Hungarian classical concert. In addition to concert performances, highly trained students take their final exams on stage, here. These performances are free - and awesome!

The **Hungarian National Opera House** is not only a landmark you should visit on your trip to Budapest, but also a perfect venue to dress up and see a world class opera or ballet performance amongst Budapest's society. Located in the middle of Andrassy Avenue, the exterior can be studied and gawked at for hours; the interiors are lavishly decorated and the foyer is the perfect place for people watching in between acts. Guided tours with mini-concerts are conducted daily. If you check at the ticket office, you can get a ticket for a performance for a very fair price. In my opinion, it has the best acoustics of any venue in the city and is definitely the most special.

Renovated and reopened in 2014, The **Erkel Theatre** is located near Keleti Palyudvar. Though not as grand as some of the other featured places, it plays hosts to some of the best shows. The opera Aida, the musical West Side Story or a symphony may be on sale. The twentieth century staid decor does not at all distract from the acoustics, staging or overall dynamics.

Duna Palota, the beautiful Neo-classical palace, has a great concert hall and is home to the Danube Symphony Orchestra, which combines classical music with Hungarian folk instruments.

The **Budapest Music Center** is located near the Central Market Hall and Corvinus University. Many of the other places embrace the classics in decor, detail and performance. This place does just the opposite. In a modern, contemporary setting, this venue hosts everything from small classical trios, jazz to modern crooners. It's innovative and chic and welcomes the like-minded.

Most musical institutions close for the summer but if that's when you're visiting us, you can still enjoy your summer evening with classical musical in open-air performances on Margaret Island during the Budapest Summer Festival.

All that Jazz...

When you think of Budapest, jazz probably doesn't come to your mind; the music that started in the American south has been and is becoming ever more popular here. Here are the best places to listen with the locals.

Jedermann Cafe

Raday utca 58, district IX. Located near the end of Raday utca, and near the 4,6 tram stop at Mester utca, this place is so popular it only takes reservations by text message. Attracting renowned bands from near and far, the music (and food) more than stands up to the hype. Wednesday is a particularly great evening to go, with regularly scheduled concerts and an open mic session for amateurs.

If Kavehaz

Raday utca 19. Also on Raday utca (less than a ten minute walk from the Kalvin Ter metro station), this place is quite cramped, but manages to be bright, warm, and inviting. Open from 11:00-24:00 with good lunch specials and moderate dinner prices. Concerts usually start at 19:30. Ask for a reservation in the upstairs gallery if you do not care to be a centimeter or too away from the featured band. I once saw a Ray

Charles cover band here. Not sure if I was tearing up due to the sensational version of 'You don't know me', because my food and wine were so good, or because of how loud it was.

Opus Jazz Club

Located in the Opus Music Center on Matyas utca 8, near Fovam Ter in district IX, this place hosts jazz concerts every Wednesday, Thursday, Friday, and Saturday at 21:00. Expect to see a variety of soloists and ensembles from around the world that may or may not fit the exact standard of jazz. Expect to mingle with Corvinus University students and many expats living in and around the new modern complexes nearby.

Epitz Pince

Ötpacsirta utca 2, district VIII, this is not a jazz club or music venue; however, on Thursday evenings (not advertised on their website, you'll just see a little poster in the window), a regular local jazz quartet plays here. They just play their hearts out for the enjoyment of the dinner guests. Because it is so close to the Hungarian National Museum, the prices are moderate with good portions. The exquisite tiled courtyard is something out of a movie. You won't know what decade or century you are in - and you won't care.

Music Festivals in Budapest

For the record, I'm not going to talk about music festivals, but about *the* music festival which I consider a must for all music enthusiasts out there. I'm talking about the Sziget Music Festival, the largest music festival in all of Europe, which is held every year on the island of Obuda in northern Budapest.

Over 1000 acts converge for one week of non-stop partying on the 266-acre island. Big bands, like Kings of Leon and Robbie Williams from a recent line, take the stage as headliners each year; but with so many stages ranging from pop to rock to electronic music, there is something for everyone. You will surely love it and won't compare it to anything else, although it is being labeled as the "European alternative to Burning Man". That is because the atmosphere and the vibe get surreal and magical and, for one week, the Obuda Island becomes the "Island Of Freedom".

So see for yourself; come to Sziget for the music and stay to visit Budapest afterwards!

Chapter 8: Budapest's Natural Treasures

Budapest is quite a busy metropolis and by now you have probably done your fair share of walking, visiting, eating, partying and what not.

If you're looking for some down time, then it's time you are introduced to Budapest's natural treasures: its many parks, zoos, and gardens. The splendor of them is what contributes to Budapest being one of the most beautiful cities in the world - the way the natural beauty compliments the man made creations of the city's spectacular architecture. The way the city is laid out, with the hill tops of Buda, the low lying Pest - a flowing river that separates the two that in itself makes for some of the most spectacular views.

If you are fortunate enough to visit the city during spring when nature is at its glory, you will not be disappointed to spend an afternoon reading a book and relaxing on a green patch of grass. In any season you'll find places of serenity in the middle of the city.

Parks

Városliget (City Park) is the largest park in Budapest and a popular weekend destination. The Park covers a wide area, great for exploring, especially those of you travelling with kids. What will you find if you do venture out exploring? How about a Castle? Vajdahunyad Castle was built for the 1896 Millenial Exhibition and you can go up to the towers and enjoy the views of the city from the top.

The park's entrance is at Heroes' Square and inside you can find just about anything you can imagine a park would have and more. Besides the aforementioned castle, there are thermal baths, meadows, sports grounds, the Gundel Restaurant (the most famous restaurant in Budapest, dating back to 1894), a time wheel, statues, memorials, esplanades and even more. You can probably complete the list when you visit it, because the park is in a state of constant change and improvement.

Gellert Hill offers its guests a huge patch of green, ideal for hiking and amazing photo ops of the expansive panorama of Budapest. No wonder that so many residents of Budapest consider it one of their favorite spots for weekend walks and exercise routines. Get lost on its winding paths that take you up the hill to "the Citadella", an old fortress built after the 1848 Revolution and commissioned by the Habsburg Monarchy. The view from the Citadella is great for admiring the city and the eight bridges over the Danube. Nearby, at the overlooks, you can make a stop at the Liberty Statue - a memorial to those who lost their life fighting for the freedom and independence of Hungary.

The next park I'll recommend happens to be my personal favorite: **Margaret Island.** The park will enchant you with a serenity contrasting the noise of the city. The island has a multitude of romantic paths to escape from the daily grind. There is an open-air amphitheater and, as recommended in the previous chapter, in the summer you can attend various opera and ballet performances during the three month long Budapest Summer Festival.

The list of fun to have on Margaret Island certainly doesn't stop there. You can rent a bike and cycle the surface of the island. There is even a shore with pools you can plunge into to reinvigorate from the heat. There are plenty of restaurants and places to get a drink and there is even a small zoo.

Additionally, the park is easily reachable by tram or bus, which stop in the middle of the Margaret Bridge (Bus 26), or you can also get there by boat. Great fun for the entire family!

A Hungarian national treasure, like the rest of Budapest, this island has something for everyone. Gardens, ancient ruins, an animal sanctuary, concert venue, and even a water tower. It alternates between being from peaceful and quiet, to vibrant and colorful (literally, the fountains are lit in various colors in synch with a musical overture). I can go on and on about it. Here's more:

It has had many names over hundreds of years, but it's been called Margaret Island since 1809. King Bela IV fled the invading Mongols in the early thirteenth century. His daughter, Princess Margaret was born in present day Croatia. Her father promised her in service to God when she was born. To fulfill that promise, upon his return to Hungary, she was raised by nuns in a convent on the island that would later be named after her. Ruins of the convent, monastery and subsequent structures are all visible on the island

Thermal waters were discovered on the western part of the island in 1866. The Danubius Health Spa Resort Margitsziget runs these thermal baths. Very upscale, but highly recommended. These baths have very specific gender hours.

The artist's garden in the middle of the island is a great place for a quiet walk. There are also forty statues of famous Hungarians, highlighting Hungary's prolificacy in the arts.

Archduke Joseph introduced three hundred species of trees to the island.

The small zoo houses about 150 animals. It has mostly small mammals, but rescued animals are also cared for here. Visitor hours are not regular, but many of the animals can be viewed from the pedestrian paths

The Margaret Island Open Air Stage opened in 1938. You're surrounded by trees, can look up to an open sky and can easily forget you're in the middle of a capital city. The seats open out like a fan and the stage is fifty metres deep.   Plays, operas, revues, as well as contemporary and classical music are all on the programme. After years or damage caused by floods the stage and performance area were completely renovated.

The Water Tower, at 57 meters, is the tallest water town in the country. It was built in 1911 and restored in 2012. It's open every day from 11:00- 22:00.

At the entrance near Margit Bridge, the Musical Fountain's water shoots streams up to fifteen metres high. From May through October, a mix of classical and contemporary music synchronizes with the water on the hour for a visual and audio spectacle.

Kopaszi Dam

This play, park and party area is treasured by those in the know in district XI. The water and surrounding waterfront was 'reclaimed' starting in 2003. The bay was dredged completely; debris and waste accumulated over decades of neglect were removed. The waterfront now has parks, a cobbled lookout point, wooden foot bridges, and pavilions. There are cafes, restaurants and playgrounds as well. Easily reached by tram number 1.

Botanical Garden & Zoo

The Budapest Zoo is one of the oldest zoo complexes in the world. It opened its doors in 1866 and it is home to over 1000 species of animals. The botanical gardens match the zoo in terms of great reviews and altogether provide an experience you shouldn't miss out on.

Unlike some other zoo parks, here the animals are well taken care of by proper zoologists. You can get really close to the animals and the kids can go to the petting zoo.

The layout is great, because it's structured according to geographical areas, which can make your visit truly informative. If you're travelling with kids make sure you include the Zoo on your itinerary, because it will be a fun outing for the entire family. The Budapest Zoo has is in the process of building two smaller family themed parks inside - The Fairy Tale Park and Pannon Park, to be completed over the next few years.

ELTE Fuveszkert

The best botanic garden in the city, and perhaps the most overlooked. Part of Eotvos University, this oasis in the middle of an often neglected area has thousands of plant species.   There's an amazing garden and water lilies able to hold a large child. An added bonus: it's open all year round. It's a twenty minute walk from the Keleti Palyaudvar. You can also take bus 99 to Koris utca.

Janos Hill, Elizabeth Lookout Tower

At 526 metres, Janos Hill (Janos Hegy) is the highest point in Budapest. On a clear day, you can see the entire city. The Erzebet (Elizabeth) lookout tower is open everyday from 8:00-20:00. Climb the winding stairs to the top of the tower. Getting there may be half the fun.

To get there, take the Zugliget Chairlift, which takes about fifteen minutes to go from one end of the hill to another. Zugliget utca 97.

The Children's Railway

Schoolchildren proudly fill various positions on and along the route. The train takes you through the best nature that Budapest has to offer. Out the window you'll see the highest hills of Buda, abandoned hideouts and fantastic scenery in addition to being on an old train run by kids.

The best way to get there is to take tram 61 from Szell Kalman ter (a stop on metro line 2) to Huvosvolgy. Follow the signs and stairs to the ticket office.

Chapter 9: Hungry in Hungary

Okay, now let's get down to business because you are probably very hungry in Hungary right now, after all that walking around. If you're wondering what to eat, you have come to the right chapter.

Budapest is undergoing a culinary revolution and restaurants and cool eateries pop up all the time, waiting to be discovered. Then there's our national cuisine, which is well represented, ranging from street food to serious multiple course dinner.

Hungarian Cuisine and Where to Eat

Let's start with the Hungarian cuisine and what separates it from others. Well, it's definitely not for people who are watching their figure. If you're into kale and broccoli, you may want to skip this part because you will definitely find it too heavy and fatty.

_t_ hold it against us, it's a mix of seasonal
ed with a history of different nationality
influences that have left a mark on our cuisine.

Our main ingredients are pork and paprika. The famous red hot paprika can be bought on a string at most farmers' markets and you can bring it home with you or as a gift for one of your foodie friends.

One of the most famous Hungarian dishes is goulash - which is made with beef, not pork. This hearty soup can trace its roots all the way back to ancient times, when it was cooked like a stew in a single pot, usually a Bograc (a traditional cooking kettle). Bogracs are still used today for outdoor cooking.

In my opinion, the best place to try an authentic goulash cooked in the Bograc is the restaurant Blue Rose, near the Synagogue on Wesselenyi utca. From outside it looks like nothing fancy, but that's the kind of place you should look for to have a real goulash. And the prices reflect just that. It's incredibly cheap for the area it's located and the meal will leave you satisfied and happy for the rest of the day or give you enough energy to go partying for the rest of the night.

Another traditional Hungarian restaurant to try is Nancsi Neni, up on the hills of Buda, a bit of a hike or a short taxi ride away. This is a famous family owned restaurant that prepares traditional dishes after secret family recipes. It has an outdoor terrace and a very friendly atmosphere, ideal for a nice lunch on Saturday and Sunday. Expect grandma style portions and don't forget to try their curd cheese dumplings. They're the rave of the town.

If you are a fan of fish, then you will love our Fisherman's Soup. And Szegedi Halászcsárda is the perfect place to have their traditional Fisherman Soup and other dishes made of fish, brought fresh. The restaurant is actually located on the banks of the Danube, with panoramic views of Gellert Hill and Buda Castle. There is also live music.

If you are planning to go there for dinner, make sure to call ahead to make a reservation and skip lunch, because the portions are huge.

For those of you that happen to be vegetarians, take heart in the fact that you too can find something to eat in Budapest. Your well-intentioned carnivorous friends, no doubt often ask you, "But what will you eat?" when you all head to dine. We try to sympathize with them - it is not easy being so close-minded. And we sincerely hope they enjoy their traditional meat dishes and stay healthy. But believe me, there is more than goulash, sausage and fried chicken to choose from.

Attesting to that fact is a dish that may be even more traditional than goulash itself. The dish is called lecso. Lecso is a thick vegetable stew. Usually the main ingredients are peppers, onions, and tomatoes. Admittedly, you have to be careful here. Some claim it is much better if you use bacon fat, but the Hungarian staple oil is sunflower and that works just as well.

Some restaurants will label it as 'Hungarian Ratatouille". If the restaurant you are at is not serving lecso, then there will still be something you can eat, such as fried mushrooms, or fried cauliflower, or fried cheese (depending on your level of vegetarianism, or commitment). The vegetarian/vegan movement is growing in Budapest. There are a handful of such restaurants now, if you want something really dedicated to the cause.

If you want to combine traditional cuisine with a historical and cultural landmark, then you should visit the New York Café, which is the most beautiful and popular coffee house in the city. Artists, writers and journalists have been calling it their home since its birth at the turn of the 20th century, and a newspaper used to be edited right on the first floor in the gallery.

After World War II, this coffee shop was turned into a sporting goods shop and in the 50's it was reopened as Hungaria. But it wasn't until 2006 that the coffee shop

...... returned to its roots. Today, the Italian Renaissance style building is a hotel and café.

The restaurant and the cigar bar are part of the hotel, but you can enjoy the Austro-Hungarian classic Menu even if you're not staying at the hotel. If you are coming to dine, you will taste delicious classics like Beef Goulash, Fish Soup, Wiener schnitzel, or Grilled Foie Gras. Or you can just grab a coffee and a Hungarian dessert like a Dobos, Sacher or Eszterházy cake. As a bonus you can try Hungarian liqueur, palinka

If you're on a budget, Budapest is abundant in street food options. While I suggest you to explore all the options while you're here, let me tell you what Hungarian street food you can expect.

You can't come to Budapest and not have a *lángos*. A lángos is a local specialty, which consists of fried flat bread with cheese and sour cream. It can also get inventive with the addition of garlic, ham and other vegetables. If you're partying in the downtown area, you can head to Akacfa utca and stop by the Langos eatery - which is open until 3 o'clock in the morning - if you can fight off the long lines of hungry crowds that it attracts.

Another great place to get lángos is at a very unassuming place near the Arany Janos utca metro station (on the M3 line). When you come up the escalators, go left outside and then immediately to your right. Next door to a gyros place, it would be easy to dismiss this as another greasy fast food place. Don't be discouraged. The lángos is great, the older man who works here is kind and the menu is in Hungarian and English

The ubiquitous crépe (or pancake) is also popular in Hungary. *Palacsinta* in Hungarian, the thin pancakes are a popular snack or meal. Coming in sweet or savory varieties, the turos palacsinta (turos being a cottage cheese variety special to Hungary) is the one to try.

If you're at Batthyany ter metro station, grab a few at Nagy Palacsinta, right across from the metro station, on the same side of the street at Spar. This place has it's menus up on a wall in both English and Hungarian. The line moves fast as the ladies working at the counter expect you to know what you want when you get to the counter.

Why have I not yet mentioned Kurtoskalacs, this staple of Hungarian street food dessert? We can call it chimney cake for the sake of convenience. Please, please, find yourself one of these cakes on a chilly day, with an appetite, at one of the many stands/stalls in and near train stations and metro stations. Look especially for the traditional outdoor charcoal grill fire baking booths that serve up this national specialty desert to dozens of hungry sweet-tooth throughout the year. Of course they taste better when the weather is right for it (during the fall and winter seasons) and when you are hungry, and when the cakes are hot and fresh.

It consists of sweet doughy bread wrapped around a wooden cylinder that is then turned on a spit over coals or next to heating elements. You can't beat the traditional charcoal version for that unmistakable authentic taste you only get from an open flame. Though if you are strapped for cash, just look outside the main halls of any of the major train stations for a booth where they will be using electric heating elements to bake these delicious concoctions. The one at Nyugati is especially popular - you can bet that there is usually a line of people waiting for their pastry personalized with a coating of sugar, cinnamon, cocoa, coconut, etc.

They are crispy on the outside and soft on the inside. And if you are handed one promptly off the spit, you see why we say 'chimney cake'. They come wrapped in a serving sleeve and steam (not to mention mouthwatering scents) escapes ascending from the upper end. They are great for sharing too. You can easily tear off pieces, reversing the direction the dough was wrapped around its cooking cylinder and then shared with others that might enjoy. But why not just get one for yourself and one for whoever you are traveling with? It really is hard to beat this unique dessert in terms of simple, down-to-earth comfort.

The culinary revolution is at its peak in Budapest and if you don't feel like having Hungarian food everyday - which I completely understand, by the way - you can find pretty much anything you can imagine in both, elegant sit-down restaurant form, or street food forms. For more options, follow and trust your nose (and the following suggestions).

For many of us, traveling is very often dramatically and majorly about food. This naturally may include fancy dinners, but who among us doesn't like a good lunch special? If you go out to eat for lunch on a regular basis, you won't be a stranger to lunch specials, but perhaps the Budapest/European method of offering lunch may benefit from a little bit of an introduction.

The lunch special in Budapest is called the napi (daily) menu. Most restaurants offer one (or two, or three) soups; two (or three, or four) entrées; and one, or two desserts. Your food might not be premium made-to-order delicacies, but leave that to fancy occasions.

Be a little bit adventurous for lunch, if not quite a bit brave. A true experience is to be had at those locations not offering a menu printed in English. But that also means you are probably getting a more authentic Hungarian experience, right?

So here are a couple of recommendations for your noon time meal.

Sas Center Etterem

Sas utca 10, district V

Located less than two minutes from the entrance to St. Stephen's Basilica, it's hard to believe that this bistro, open exclusively for lunch would offer local prices in such a tourist heavy place. For a fair price get the soup and main dish of the day. Open from 11:00- 15:00, all its tables are in a covered outdoor terrace.

Benczur Haz Etterem

Benczur utca 27, district VI

Lunch before or after a trip through Heroes' Square. Take a walk down this quaint tree lined street to this cafe and restaurant. Open until 15:00

Fecske Presszo

Baross utca 10, district VIII

Take a slight detour off Raday utca and head to this place a few steps away from the Szabo Ervin Library. It gets packed by university students and businessmen around lunchtime. Sit outside seating for great people watching. Lunch specials are from 12:00 - 17:00. A great place for a meal, coffee, or drinks outside of the lunch special, if you don't mind loud music and dim lighting.

Menta Terasz

Margit korut 14, district II

A clean and beautiful dining room right in the heart of Buda, near the Margit Bridge. Their napi menu includes a soup, main dish and dessert. During warmer months, I recommend you to enjoy your meals in the back garden.

Mongolian BBQ

Marvany utca 19/a, district II

Don't let the name discourage you from thinking you won't get an authentic local experience. This place, offering a full buffet and made to order grilled dishes (which are all excellent, by the way), also has a delicious napi menu.

If you are one of those who can be somewhat overwhelmed after several days of everything which you are not used to, and are in the mood for some of the more traditional international cuisine, then the following is what you should be looking for in the heart of Budapest.

Thai food

There are at least two Thai food restaurants that have become chains in the city center. The one you should really try is called Pad Thai Wok 2 Go. It has a location on Gozdu Udvar (which is Budapest's largest, busiest alleyway/lane) and another on October 6th Street. Their menu is streamlined, the ingredients are high quality, and the chefs (it seems) are all Thai themselves. You can pick from six or more noodle bases, plenty of toppings (different meats, tofu, and vegetables), and then pick from one of six different Asian style sauces.

The prep cooks hand the chefs all your ingredients, which are quickly whisked together in front of your eyes in a powerfully hot wok, behind a glass pannel. I strongly recommend the Indonesian Satay sauce –it's delicious!

Wok 2 Go is a little bit better than its competitor, Buddha Wok, even if Buddha has more locations on the Grand Boulevard.

If you are in the mood for good sushi, you may get disappointed in Budapest. There is one popular chain of all-you-can-eat system dining called Wasabi, but the it is often overloaded with filler items that everyone just watches pass by while waiting for real sushi pieces. It is especially challenging if you are waiting for vegetarian sushi options. One can only eat so many small trays of bean sprouts and kimchi. However, Wasabi does sport a couple of great beers from the Munich brewery Paulaner.

Hummus Bar

Now, how about some Middle Eastern food? You can throw a stone in Budapest and it will hit one Turkish kebab place, and bounce off and hit another Turkish kebab place. They all smell quite delicious and the steady stream of customers testifies to their appeal. However, here is where you should go for something just a cut above the rest: Hummus Bar.

Even though it has more and more locations sprouting up throughout the metropolitan Budapest area, it has not lost even a small step in its commitment to simple, delicious, affordable Middle Eastern fare. The shawarma smells great, but go ahead and try the vegetarian options. Hummus Bar fries up little crispy falafel balls that are seasoned just right every time someone places an order. There is no reheating here, oh no. You will reward yourself even more if you go to their location on October 6th street, which boasts a daily continuously functioning fresh laffa oven. It is worth just to go there and smell the dozens of fresh breads the single baker churns out all day long for his hungry patrons. With just a slight char around the edges, it is the perfect platform to wrap around your sandwich ingredients. What is more, the staff always greets you with a complimentary glass of lemonade (summertime) or mint tea (wintertime).

Mexican (avoid)

You might lose count of the number of so-called 'Mexican' restaurants once you walked into in the Budapest city center just hoping for a decent burrito or taco - only to be sorely disappointed and left asking "why do they even try?" This is not meant to disparage anyone who is working hard to serve food at such a place. Rather, just keep in mind that if you are determined to get Mexican food in Budapest, it will quite probably not be like anything that you might consider authentic or truly enjoyable, especially if you have been to Mexico, California, Texas, New York, or anywhere else in the States. So it is emphatically recommended to curb one's Mexican cravings until arriving at a more favorable locale.

Coffee

Wow, we have already considered so many avenues of good eats in Budapest, yet we really haven't even begun to scratch the surface of - none other than - coffee!

Okay, some will say the best cappuccino or espresso in Europe is to be had in Italy; they may be right, if taste is truly an objective science. But let's just be nice to ourselves and each other, say it is subjective, and move on. That way it is much easier to let oneself enjoy the myriad of cafe options available in Budapest. Without further ado, let's start at the top and see how far we can get before time might fail us.

Cafe Frei

You simply must visit any Cafe Frei at least once. If you enjoy coffee - maybe even if you don't - you will definitely plan a return journey after perusing and enjoying any of their broad offerings. The selection is huge, encompassing all (I mean it - All) varieties of coffee from the four corners of the earth.

Go ahead, play it safe, order a classic Italian cappuccino. You will enjoy it, absolutely. You will probably want another. But then take another look at the menu, which is arranged as a world map on the wall behind the barista's station in each Cafe Frei location. Just try an Arabic coffee - cooked in copper pots on a hot bed of sand - or something from the Caribbean, South America, or Africa. Not to mention East Asia!

This place is one of a kind, and it eclipses by far any of the other chains available (not giving any names, but they just so happen to rhyme with Starbucks, Costa Coffee, and California Coffee Company.) Don't even bother with the other chains, even if you want a taste of home, or even if you are feeling particularly pop-culture/mass-consumer brainwashed. Just go to Frei, it is as simple as that. The one at the south end of Vaci Utca (a hop, skip, and a jump away from the Central Market Hall) is the best. It also offers a nice variety of special cocktails.

The Book Cafe

The two-level bookstore on Andrassy Avenue is briefly mentioned elsewhere in this guide, but here is where we get to the really great part about it. Head up just one more story from the second level of the bookstore (which incidentally has great historical Budapest photo album books) and enter a royally decked out hall, all prepared just for you to enjoy a cup of coffee or tea. You may even go at the right time to be serenaded as there is a grand piano in the middle of the room.

The name of this place is Book Cafe, but don't get it mixed up with its several smaller cousins scattered around at other Alexandra Bookstore locations in Budapest. While all those smaller cafes also serve a great cup of coffee in comfortable environs, if you only have time to go to one, this should be the one.

Try not to be disappointed in the lack of historical significance. The building was a casino, then a department store, and now has been converted as you see it. But if you still want to pretend to be going there to sip coffee with nobility, we won't tell.

Auguszt

The Auguszt Cukrászda is on Kossuth Lajos Avenue (the same street as Rakoczi Avenue), near Astoria and Ferenciek Square. It's one of the oldest cafes in the city of Budapest. This is a really great location to enjoy a perfectly crafted latte or cappuccino. The interior is beautiful, with great floor-to-ceiling artwork on the wall to your right as you walk in, and a chandelier that looks like it belongs in a royal palace. They also have handmade marzipan treats molded into various animals, dolls, etc.

If you are in the mood for something sweet, definitely order their cream cake. It will be an instant classic for you, as it has been for generations before you and I. And one of the best things about places like this - you can sit for hours and no one will bother you. Bring a book, write emails, or whatever you want. You can make yourself at home and not feel like you should be compelled to leave. Opens at 10:00, and is closed on Sunday. There is also a second location in Buda.

Urania Cafe

Located between Astoria and Blaha Lujza on Rakoczi street, I cannot understand why this place isn't more popular. Maybe many don't know that you don't have to attend a film (the cafe is on the upper level of a movie house) to sit in the cafe. Walk up a spiral staircase and enjoy the lovely accented interior and a view of the street - very likely all by yourself.

Aztek Choxolat

The name is not a typo. Hopefully it heightens your curiosity. Its timeless courtyard setting? The friendly service? Inventive seasonal flavors of chocolate and coffee? It's all of that and more. It's a tiny place, so prepare to take it on the go or sit outside before heading out to explore this place - in a location close to Astoria. I encourage you to peek into other open courtyards and passageways throughout the city.

Gerbaud

Cafe Gerbeaud is located right at Vorosmarty ter. Often mentioned as one of the best coffeehouses in all of Europe, it's one of the largest in Budapest. The place continues the proud traditions of the man whose name it bears. The cakes are great, but what's really great here is the ice cream. If you want the ultimate five star cafe experience in Budapest, this is it. Note the main influences of the interior like the French tables and Austrian chandeliers. They take everything seriously - the decor, the coffee, the service. Don't mind all the tourists, just enjoy it.

Street Festivals

Any guidebook about Budapest would be sorely incomplete without mentioning its many holiday markets and street festivals. Many of these festivals center around one specific food or beverage item. Oktoberfest is just one among a number of beer festivals. There should also be another one during the summer months somewhere in City Park with a huge variety of Hungarian, Czech, German and Belgian beers. There are also wine festivals, palinka festivals, chocolate festivals, and generic street festivals on certain holidays - or at times just for the fun of it.

One of the most popular street festivals takes place in the heat of summer and sees the entire length of Andrassy Avenue shut down to traffic (other than the thundering herds of hungry and thirsty fairgoers). This festival also provides a multitude of interactive booths for young and old alike. Everyone seems to like the large number of public buses parked and available to tour. There are also games, face painting, and a raconteur for the kids. Head all the way to Heroes' Square and City Park to see the festival spread out even more. There is a horse parade and a temporary medieval style archery training range set up near Vajdahunyad Castle.

By the way, let's mention some of the food available at these street festivals. You will be sure to stumble across fresh sausages, fried potatoes (skillet style, pommes frites style, and chip style), langos and kurtoskalacs, handmade chocolates and candies (and marzipan), and dozens of other options, traditional and international. You should look for something that might be labeled as 'bread langos'. It is essentially super fresh pizza, handcrafted before your very eyes, adorned with tasty ingredients such as red onions, sausage, fresh cheese, etc. The pizzas are baked in square iron pans inside a clay oven with wood logs burning at the bottom. Stand back for a few minutes and watch the craftsmen at work, especially the guy running the oven. He is clearly familiar with his craft and it is obvious that he has turned out more than a pizza pie or two in his day. Enjoy your delicious turn as his customer.

The trendy urban food truck scene is getting up on its feet now in Budapest, and it is especially making its presence known at these street festivals, but you will still be hard pressed to find food trucks at lunch time otherwise. It is still not anywhere close to find them easily as it is in some urban areas in the States, and elsewhere. So have a gander and see what you find, if the abundance of delicious traditional options just isn't enough for you.

Around the year-end holiday season, there is a great street market at Kalvin Ter. They have all of the afore-mentioned favorites, as well as one that is particularly special to colder weather that deserves a moment of its own mention here - and that is hot mulled wine. Nothing that you can sip out of a cup warms you up more appealingly on a cold damp winter evening or afternoon. Speaking of wine, check out Chapter 9 below for some more great tips and insights about this topic.

Chapter 10: Wine In Budapest

Did you know Hungary has some world-class vineyards? If you didn't, now you do, so make sure you don't leave the capital without indulging in some of the finest wine tastings there are.

There are many wine cellars, wine shops, and places to go for a real wine tasting experience. Here are my favorite spots.

Faust Cellar is part of the large labyrinth of caves located underneath the Buda Hills. There are around 200 caves underneath Budapest, which were formed due to the thermal springs, and three of them are open to the public. This is what makes Faust cellar such a must during your vacation here. That and the fact that the owners, a young couple, provide a wonderful, personalized experience for their guests. You can reach it from the lobby Hilton Hotel, going down quite a few stairs until you get to the basement. Make sure to book in advance because the place is very small and has only four tables, but it's worth it. You get to try a multitude of wines and the owners describe each one in a candle-lit atmosphere.

Wine and Cruise is a great place to get your magical evening in Budapest started. This wine tasting takes place during a cruise down the Danube and takes you on a journey through some of the most famous wine vineyards. The views that will accompany each sip of wine make a very low price feel like a bargain for what you're getting. During the one hour and a half cruise you will get to go through 7 types of Hungarian wines and, if you haven't had enough, you can buy some of the bottles on board.

If you're more of a wine lover than a party goer, and you are looking for a nice little wine bar to enjoy your evening, you will be pleased with the many options of wine bars scattered throughout the city, ranging from cheaper local pubs to more select expensive ones.

Galleria 12 is a little wine bar on the Buda side, which combines "wine with pictures" in exhibits of the art of local artists. It's a small but intimate locale with great wines and a small but excellent food menu to compliment your choice of wine.

Doblo is located on the corner of Dob and Hollo Streets and has an impressive collection of both mainstream and lesser-known wineries. They stand out because they always have a band playing to accompany you in your night of wine adventures and also hold wine tastings. To go with your wine, you can choose from their meat and cheeses plates, which include some exquisite smoked meats, pickles, and breads.

As an alternative to the wine bars, new concepts are popping up in Budapest as we speak. A unique one is the Champagne bar. If you're curious about it, go to Zizi Bubbles and Tapas, which is the first champagne themed bar in Budapest that focuses on providing the customers with a variety of bubbles and tapas. The list of sparkling wine is endless and includes a lot of high quality Hungarian sparkling and foaming wine. The tapas are both Spanish and Hungarian. Zizi Bubbles and Tapas is located close to St. Stephen Basilica and occasionally has live music playing.

Do you want to bring some fine wine back home with you as souvenirs and as gifts for your friends and family? Then you will find yourself with plenty of options. If you don't mind spending (that is, overspending) a few dollars, simply look around at any variety of souvenir shops. You are sure to find great gifts. If, however, you are travelling on a budget, or simply don't want to waste money, then here is a great tip: go to the grocery store! Grocery stores in Budapest have plenty of decent wine to choose from that will not hurt your pocketbook, even if you choose to buy two or three bottles. And don't be put off by self proclaimed wine enthusiasts who claim that no good wine can be bought unless it is from a boutique wine shop. Sure, you have a much better chance of receiving good tips and advice from the shopkeepers in wine specialty stores, but a little self-confidence and label examination can go a long way towards getting good wine at great prices. For example, check out the selection at any Tesco. (In case you don't know, Tesco is a supermarket chain from the UK, and it is popular across Europe. Budapest has a plethora of them, both large ones on the outskirts of the city center, and the smaller Tesco 'Express' is peppered across the city.)

If you want something that might be a little harder to find in your hometown, you should give Egri Bikaver a try. This is a blend from the Eger wine region. Bikaver translates into English as "Bull's Blood". We might never be sure why they chose such a moniker, but this blended wine is suitable for anyone who enjoys wine even a tiny bit. What is even better, you can easily find a bottle to fit any budget. As mentioned above, even spending only a few Euros per bottle can get you a wine you will really enjoy! A good rule of thumb may be to look for bottles that actually have a description of the wine or the winery on the label. That should help ensure you will be happy with the final product.

A last quick side note about wine in Budapest: wine spritzers are very popular. Hungarians call them 'froccs' (pronounced something like 'frootch'). They come in a wide array of wine to seltzer ratios and can be made with white or red wine (also rosé makes a refreshing summer froccs).

As mentioned earlier, in the winter, mulled or hot wine is very popular. You'll see it being sold at markets and cafes everywhere. However, my favorite place for this is completely out of the box. It's a hole in the wall with a yellow sign inside Keleti Station. It's next to a stand selling second hand books.

Chapter 11: Shopping Scene

Budapest is a major metropolis, and like every metropolis you can find just about anything brand wise. There are plenty of large shopping malls to choose from, of course, which you can easily find back home. So let's focus for a few moments on something you will not find back home. The two most famous streets for shopping in Budapest are Vaci Utca and Andrássy Avenue.

Váci utca is the single most famous street in Budapest. It has long been a major attraction in Budapest and it welcomes tourists to the pedestrian street with restaurants, cafes and lots and lots of shopping. It offers luxury shops, boutiques and your regular Zaras, H&Ms, and whatnots. The street is also full of historical monuments and plaques commemorating the past. For example, at house number nine on the street is an old inn, where Mozart gave a concert at the age of eleven. You can reach the street by tram number 2, which runs parallel to the Danube, so whenever you feel like it, you can take one of the side streets and dash away to the river in an effort to escape the Vaci Utca crowds. If you get hungry while shopping but don't want to pay the "top dollar prices" of the Vaci Utca restaurants geared towards wide eyed tourists, you should know that the street ends opposite the Central Market Hall. So, build up an appetite and then go to the market and hit the food stands for some cheap and hearty Hungarian dishes.

Andrássy Avenue is where the Opera House is located and, if you didn't pack a gown to attend the opera, this is the street to shop for one - and buy one if your pocketbook can handle it. The street is abundant in designer shops like Gucci, Armani, and Roberto Cavalli, built similarly to an elegant boulevard in Paris which it connects the city center with City Park and Heroes' Square. There are many luxury shops, old school restaurants, atmospheric cafes, and even a wonderful two-story bookstore. The avenue is lined with beautiful architecture that will enchant you on your walk, but if you are wondering if there is anything else to do but shop and eat, there is also the Museum of Terror, where you can learn about the country's history during the Nazi occupation and Communist Era.

Paloma is located on Kossuth Lajos Street 14-16 (on the Pest side), which used to be the shopping street of Budapest. Residents would head here to purchase everything they needed. When shopping malls came into being, Kossuth Lajos Street became less popular and now it's just a big street with stores that barely make it from month to month.

If you want to experience something very creative and rejuvenating in the midst of the commercial uncertainty - visit Paloma. Paloma has high aspirations to bring back the golden age of Lajos Street. Its name invokes the memories of what the street once was and the innovation of Hungary's millennials. The concept is different and it aims to be a contemporary centre composed of Hungarian design boutiques and gallery spaces. You can see designers hard at work drawing, sewing, and hopefully selling. They welcome visitors and questions. If you want to see or have something unique from your travel, definitely head here.

It takes advantage of its location in a beautiful classic building, showcasing the courtyards that are so frequently hidden behind old facades. Meet the young designers from the Hungarian industry, and pick up a hand crafted product. There are dozens of small shops selling everything from clothes, bags, jewelry, shoes, to decorative pieces and more.

Bolhapiac's exact location - Zichy Mihaly utca 14 - is a truly one-of-a-kind shopping experience adding to the allure of Varosliget (City Park), a large flea market where pros and locals sell all kinds of *everything*.

Although it is a large imposing structure deep in the park, you'll really get to know the people on a personal level. The easiest way to get there is to take the m1 to Mexikoi utca and start walking into the park in a southeast direction.

Although it may not seem suitable for an insider's guide to include this, it's impossible not to - Budapest has one of the highest concentrations of malls, for the size of its population, than any other capital in Europe. What's more, the majority of the people there are Hungarians. It's an interesting phenomenon. Here's a breakdown of the ones you may find most useful for your trip, what is unique about them, and some extra tips and info.

Every mall has a large grocery store inside. If you are renting an apartment and would like to cook and have beer, wine, beverages, water, or snacks at your accommodations, the grocery stores in the mall often have better prices than the smaller stores outside (Lidl and Aldi also have better prices for these items).

Also if you left a charger or some essential electronic item at home, the malls usually have either a Euronics or MediaMarkt, which tend to have all of these items.

MOM Park is a nice place to orient yourself before heading up into the tonier sections of the Buda Hills. This is the place to be if you want to see Hungarians from the suburbs, business people, and diplomats who have planted roots here, all mixed with the locals from Buda.

The movie theatre features movies in English - with Hungarian subtitles. Most theatres dub Hungarian over English, so it's important to check. It's not far from Deli Train Station.

The surrounding area is green, bright, and quiet. Explore the surrounding hills for some of the prettiest, most exclusive smaller cafes in the city.

At the other end of Buda is Allee. Located at the Ujbuda-Kozpont station of the M4 line, it's bustling and convenient. The usual suspects are there, but also the the very best of Hungary's chain cafes - Cafe Frei and Cserpes Tejivo. There is a local market right next to this mall with vendors from the countryside selling fresh produce. It's also a few tram stops away from Gellert.

West End mall is located directly behind Nyugati Train Station in Pest. Reachable on the M3 metro line and at the halfway point of the 4,6 tram between Oktogon and the Pest side of Margaret Island.

The best part of this mall is that the roof is open. There is a garden, playground, and esplanades for lovers and recluses alike. Go to the top floor and look for the carefully marked stairs to the roof. It's an honest view of the sixth and thirteenth districts. You'll be sharing the rooftop with teenagers, a few families, Hilton staff members and those of us who aren't the best shoppers.

With one of the most extensive food courts of any mall in Budapest on its lower level, it's a very good choice if you are with a group, or kids, and everyone wants something different. Hungarian, Indian, Greek, Italian, and Chinese are just some examples of the types of food you'll find here. There's a Spar inside, an Aldi across the street, and a Lidl not far away.

Arena is ten to fifteen walk from Keleti Train Station. One of the largest malls in the country, it welcomes you with an ice skating rink in front. It's often packed, as it has something for everyone. The set-up seems to make everyone feel upscale, despite there being a lot of budget friendly stores and services. If you need to load up on goods, this is the place to go.

There isn't just one Mammut. There is two. Mammut I and Mammut II are connected by an above ground covered bridge. Smaller boutiques, that stood the test of time, and large chain stores co-exist in this mega complex near the Szell Kalman metro station. The 4,6 tram stops in front. This mall has a lot of style and more importantly seems to have more restaurants and small shops open than others on Sunday. There's a standout Greek restaurant here. To highlight how the old and new coexist and Budapest, the Fény Utca Market Hall is located directly behind this mall.

Corvin Mall is located at the Corvin-Negyed M3 metro station and at a 4,6 tram stop. Before you even get to the entrance, feel free to stop at a Cserpes Tejivo, wine bar, movie theater, and second hand shop. There's a CBA grocery store on the lower level and a small but notable food court on the top level. There is an Alexandra bookstore inside. As with all of the Alexandra book shops in Budapest, there is a cafe inside. The one in Corvin stands out as it in the basement level. Have a glass of wine or coffee, in a cozy, quiet setting surrounded by books.

Behind the mall is a pedestrian walkway with more restaurants and cafes. Just a few blocks more, you'll leave the sleek and modern area and be in the middle of grittier housing complexes. Explore the area to get a different, perhaps more realistic view of life for many residents.   Hopefully you'll get to also experience their warmth and sincerity.

Koki Terminal is located at the terminus of the m3 line, Kobanya Kispest. You'll get to this station if you take the 200E to the airport. If you need to pick up something, kill time, or even enjoy some great coffee, you won't have to go far.

Chapter 12: Nightlife

Budapest has one of the most electrifying (okay, maybe that is a tad subjective) nightlives in the world. If you're here on a trip, I recommend you dance all night long at least once, if you are into that sort of thing, of course.

There is no particular district designated to this type of entertainment and a good time can come out of just about anywhere in the city. The choices are basically unlimited: pubs, dance clubs, jazz bars, casinos, and the new wave in entertainment - the ruin bars (which get their own chapter, see below). The nightlife charms you with unique decors, modern vibes, old architecture, and late night hours. If you happen to travel to Budapest during the summer, then the nights will get even longer and the options will become even more endless, from festivals to outdoor venues, to parties on the Danube or free concerts in the many parks. You may just stumble upon a quiet bistro with dancing in a backyard.

Here are some of my recommendations for clubs in the city, but don't be limited to this simple guide book's list. Be flexible, be spontaneous, and get yourself inspired by the captivating ambiance to discover your own little piece of heaven.

The **Fono Budai Zenehaz** (Fono Music Hall) is a great place to hear live bands representing the Balkans, Romania and Hungary. There is a careful curation of workshops, performances, and concerts, with the understanding and the urgency for everyone involved - to just dance. It's very easy to reach by taking tram number   1.

A38 has long been a traditional stop on the nightlife scene in Budapest. It's a great place to grab a drink, have some food, and enjoy one of the many concerts and events happening on the boat. That's right; the club is on the beautiful Danube inside an old Ukrainian stone-carrier. It has three floors - the roof, a restaurant and a club. My recommendation is you check out the weekly spin-off "Random Trip", which is every Tuesday and the line-up changes constantly. The music is diverse and ranges from pop, underground, funk, alternative, electronic, and dance.

Peaches and Cream on Nagymezo Street is another hot spot inside a magnificent location on a thriving street. Plan to spend time here if you want to spend a little bit of money and be treated like royalty. This is the place in Budapest to get a VIP table, colorful cocktails and party in style in a high class atmosphere with a cool, international crowd of people. You'll be dancing to RƏB and retro tunes until the wee hours of the morning.

Morrison's 2 is a cheaper alternative than the first two, but a great club nonetheless. Located among upscale restaurants, hotels and grand residential buildings near the Margaret Bridge, the venue includes various stages and rooms, and even a karaoke section. The cocktails are great and they are pretty cheap even for us locals. Enjoy drink specials with salsa, reggae, and pop tunes along with a young and international crowd.

Trafiq is a combination between the trending ruin pubs and the fancier establishments of the downtown area. Trafiq is quickly becoming the hottest club in town, resulting in long queues to get in, even on weekdays. The live acts are really worth it. I'm not aware of any other club that is as inventive in its musical curation and has a DJ with a violinist and a vocalist entertaining the massive crowd. If you decide to go, make sure you go there early or book ahead unless you don't mind the endless line.

Chapter 13: The Budapest Experience - Best "Ruin Pubs"

Many cities would hide somewhat crumbling, blights of buildings from everyone. What does Budapest do? Turns them into a bar, of course.

An authentic Budapest experience is going out to "a ruin bar". These open air (or closed air, we won't be partial) bars provide an excellent alternative to the nightclub outings because their retro atmospheres create a great vibe. The ruin bars are transformed from abandoned (or very much so lived-in) buildings in Budapest and they attract mixed public.

You'll find some of the best beers in ruin pubs and also idiosyncratic characters and nonchalant decor to accompany them. Some are more 'ruined' than others, so keep looking until you find one you like. There is a concentration of ruin pubs in district VII.

Try the following suggestions which, many would agree, should be at the top of any recommendation list:

Eleszto is located at Tuzolto Street 22, near Corvin Plaza. It's one off the beaten path choice and exactly what a ruin pub is and should be. There is no brightly lit sign or advertisements out front. Chances are you may walk past it a couple of times before you realize you have found the building you are looking for.

When you go in, take a right to the bar at the back. You will be greeted with an appetizing selection of probably at least ten tap beers, running the full spectrum of styles. Feel free to ask the bartenders for descriptions, tips, suggestions, and happily, samples. Eleszto is by no means a quiet place, so go early if you just want to drink your beer in peace. Later in the evening, expect yourself to be elbowing through loud crowds just to get to the bar to order.

At times, some pubs take certain liberties with the 'ruin' concept (i.e. more or less broken chairs, tables that are so wobbly you really cannot set your beer down, floors with obstacles, course-like trip hazards, apparently intentionally chilly drafts during cold weather. Eleszto is not immune to this, although it does seem that they are at least shoring things up for safety's sake. But if you know what you are getting yourself into, then ruin pubs are just the place for you. The advantage is that oftentimes you get really great beers while being able to avoid the pretense and formality of traditional establishments. We just hope this peculiarity does not become so popular that it turns into a style that everyone think is original. Rhetoric aside, just enjoy your beer.

Hopfanatic, is located at Hunyadi ter 11, just a block down from Andrassy Avenue. Yeah, about enjoying your beer…go to Hopfanatic, just go! It is not nearly as hip and trendy as its rivals, but it more than makes up for that with the best beers in Budapest, hands down when it comes to Hungarian micros.

All of the beer here comes from the same micro-brewery. You can find them on tap from time to time at other pubs too, but they are cheaper here. And they are all in one place. They usually have ten or so on tap. If you go frequently, no doubt you will find one or two favorites - there is bound to be worthy substitutes.

As far as style is concerned, while you do have a few hand paintings on the walls of the basically one-room basement, the decor and atmosphere is not really about aesthetics or comfort per se. But know that what it is really about is good, good, good beer. There is a great chance it will not be crowded early on and you and your party may even have the place to yourselves. Sometimes they play B.B. King, and other decent music rather than the pop/techno that is so frequent other places. Good beer just washes down better to good tunes, doesn't it? Sit and relax as long as you please. The wifi signal is better than Eleszto's.

Don't expect to be waited on, you will need to walk up to the bar each time. Oh, and the staff does not expect to be tipped either.

You cannot go wrong with Eleszto or Hopfanatic, but just in case you are curious, there are plenty of others to choose from. Here are a few more suggestions.

Kertem, Olof Palme sétány 3. It is located in the middle of Varosliget, where you can enjoy a beer in the shade of the park's trees. You are near a garden, by a zoo, a stone's thrown from a centuries old castle, and thermal baths - welcome to Budapest.

Pótkulcs, Csengery utca 65/b. Not far from Nyugati train station and West End shopping center, don't let the rough exterior prevent you from feeling like you're in a friends old flat.

Udvar Rom, Klauzál u. 21. A good spot to start exploring an area that has embraced this phenomenon. It's all about locals and all about good beer.

Mazel Tov, Akacfa utca 47. Although it meets the definition of a ruin pub, it's so gorgeous, and well designed it seems unfair to include it with more of the 'rougher' locations. Great beer, great music, family friendly and a 'can't go wrong' menu.

Instant. While the phrase "ruin bar" has become a phenomenon in the Budapest nightlife, there is one bar that is deemed the most popular. Instant bar is a maze of rooms - over 23, 6 bars, 4 dance floors, and it also has an underground basement for concerts and performances. It is surreal, different, and it has some of the most unusual decorations and artwork on display. Plus, the beers are cheap and the staff is friendly.

Corvintető is the place to go if you want to experience the true underground (ironically it is situated on top of a building) scene of going out in Budapest. It's a vibrant place, on a rooftop on top of the Corvin department store; the views will compliment that nice and cheap cold beer. The best day to go is Saturday night, after midnight, but don't dress up - the atmosphere is very chill. Also, be aware of your surroundings when you get to the club, the area is not exactly squeaky clean.

Dürer Garden is in the old building of the University, Faculty of Arts. It is one of the best rock bars, which often has punk or rock concerts - so check their schedule. Otherwise, you will find general good fun, a football table, darts, a courtyard, and good music and vibes.

Szimpla Kert is the trendsetter, the original ruin bar. Located in the Jewish Quarter, next to the Great Synagogue, this bar is simply a must and it is happening any night of the week. You won't regret your visit to Szimpla and its genre-defining vibe. The artwork displayed is eclectic and the maze of rooms will keep you busy for the rest of the night, while you enjoy one of the friendliest and most casual atmospheres in the nightlife of Budapest.

Kuplung is located inside a former garage on the fabulous street of Kiraly Utca. The decoration is funk with an "under the sea" motif and, if you go on Monday, all drinks are half off.

Chapter 14: Sleeping - Luxury at Affordable Prices

Budapest is in no shortage of accommodation options for tourists from all walks of life. There are luxury hotels, budget friendly hotels, business oriented hotels, historical hotels, hostels, apartments for rent, and so on and so forth. Even the high-end hotels are more affordable than those you might find in Western Europe. However, summers get trickier because of the wave of tourists and prices tend to shoot up 20 or 30%.

In this chapter, I am going to recommend one hotel from each category. My recommendation is based on my personal experience with the hotel, location, reviews, buzz, and historical importance.

Historical Hotels

In Budapest you can stay in a building of historical importance and beautiful architecture for a fraction of what these hotels would cost in other places in Europe. Have you ever tried to book a room at Carlton in Cannes? No? Well, don't bother. Instead of going to France, come to Budapest and live luxuriously in the mansions of yesteryear.

My Recommendation

And the winner is....Hotel Palazzo Zichy. A boutique hotel that transformed its interiors into state of the art contemporary style, but originally built in the 19th century for a famous Hungarian noble, Count Nandor Zichy, who used it as a personal family residence until his death. It's perfect for a romantic trip and located in a quiet square in the Budapest Palace quarter, conveniently tucked away from the Grand Boulevard crazy traffic and bustle.

Honorable mention goes to...Maison Budapest, located on Andrassy. The best of Budapest is right outside your door. Walk to City Park or stroll down Andrassy, or the parallel Varosliget Fasor, for one of the best walks to take you from quiet architectural bliss to the pulsing center centre.

Budget Friendly Hotels

Don't worry if you can't afford accommodation in one of the 5 star hotels located in those enormous palaces. You can still have all the comfort you need because the city of Budapest is literally abundant in choices when it comes to budget friendly hotels. And don't worry about being pushed to the outskirts of the city like in other European capitals. You can get a 3 star hotel room in the center of Budapest for a really fair price.

My Recommendation

City Ring Hotel is located off the Grand Boulevard, close to Margaret Island and the Parliament building, and virtually all the good areas for going out. This comfortable 3 star hotel will offer just the basic accommodation but in a perfect location that can't be beat.

Hostels

Hostels are not only ideal for saving money but, in my opinion, are one of the best ways to travel if you want to meet other international travelers. Especially if you're not too keen on overpaying for needless comforts indoors when the real adventure is outside your hotel room. Hostels are aplenty in Budapest and popular amongst the youthful travelers that come to our city to experience the incredible art and music scene. You don't have to worry about their locations; many of these hostels have a better placement or are on the same block that the 5 star hotels.

My Recommendation

The Best Choice Hostel is exactly what it preaches: the best choice hostel. It's located on the most vibrant and famous street in Budapest, Vaci Utca. The reviews are through the roof. People seem to be really enjoying their stay and the owner, Levi, is a very helpful guide.

There are many options in Budapest unlike in Communist times, when there would've been only a few state owned hotels in very grey, unwelcoming conditions. Now the market has spoken and the competition is fierce. So do your due diligence and find the best deals to fit your budget, mood, and travelling experience. Just make sure you book ahead of time.

Chapter 15: Daytrips Outside of Budapest

Szekesfehervar

The first capital of Hungary dates back to the ninth century and was founded by prince Geza. You'll find Szekesfehervar to be a vibrant but calmer respite to Budapest. It has at least one each of what Budapest has to offer - ruins, a castle, a pedestrian square, museums, passageways with local shops and businesses, a mall, and thermal baths. All are within an easy walk of each other. You can spend a few hours or a day here.

In a couple of hours, I found an empty cafe serving great Irish coffee - a tiny bar off a side street, decorated as or that may have perhaps been the parlor of a stately family that quickly filled with grandmas and twenty somethings. The city embraces the old and new with no pretense.

Take the train from Deli Palyaudvar to be here in 45 minutes. It's about a twenty walk or a five minute bus ride directly from the train station to the city center. The bus station is closer to the city center.

It's on the way to Lake Balaton and cities to the south. Definitely worth a look or break from the larger cities.

Eger

Possessing over a thousand years of history, castles, ruins, and churches this place has some landmarks that hold Budapest's rich history. As one of the hillier cities in Hungary, exploring the city center brings varied vantage points from the heights (especially in the districts east of the castle) that face the center and Bukk Mountains.

Even with its history and bucolic surroundings, Eger is known primarily for its wine and spirits. The popular Egri Bikaver is produced here. The two hundred year old Istvan wine cellar doesn't discriminate - it is home to wines from Hungary's twenty wine regions.

There are buses every hour to Budapest and Inter-city trains. The trip is about two hours each way. If you are feeling adventurous, travel a few kilometers more to Egerszalok. It is famous for Europe's only salt hill and another city sitting on a wealth of thermal springs. It's an easy trip to the Saliris Resort and Spa with its indoor & outdoor pools and saunas. Passes are available for the day or a few hours, and it is open year round.

Szentendre

One of the easier and most popular day trips outside of Budapest is a nice way to spend a few hours if you need or want a break from the city, without the effort of the other choices. From the Batthyany ter metro station take the green HEV to Szentendre. The ride goes along the Danube, going past Obuda, as well as the islands and peninsulas sandwiched between Buda and Pest to the north of the city.

From the station, it's a pleasant fifteen minute walk to the Danube Promenade and main pedestrian areas of the city. Among the many cafes and shops (including many where you can find well made Hungarian handicrafts). Cafe Dorothea off the main path is a standout.

Esztergom

Another former capital of Hungary, this stunning city sits on the Danube right across from Slovakia. Its Basilica is the largest in Hungary. The structure and surrounding fortress make for an impressive hike and view over one of the oldest cities in Hungary. The winding streets below, along with centuries old architecture add to this historic charm of the area.

After decades of damage and destruction, efforts were made to restore the place in the mid twentieth century. Excavations on the site continue adding to the cultural value of the region.

There are excellent cafes and restaurants throughout the city. The staff, as in many places of Budatest, tends to be helpful and warm.

You can reach Esztergom by taking a bus from the Arpad hid (Arpad Bridge) bus terminal, located outside the Arpad hid metro station.

Even better, take a beautiful ride up the Danube, along the bend, dotted with lush hills and small villages by taking a train from Nyugati Palyaudvar to Sturovo, Slovakia.

Sturovo, located directly across the river from Esztergom, is in itself part of the adventure. When getting off the train, you may think you've been fooled and stepped into an empty, neglected town. But don't be fooled by the first impression. A short walk to the left of the station and you'll start to see the impressive former capital of Hungary come into view. The walk through town is at least forty five minutes. Walk through the mostly Hungarian speaking town and over the bridge that connects Sturovo to Esztergom. The recently rebuilt bridge offers stunning views of the imposing complex on the Hungarian side, and the tranquil section of the Danube.

Visegrad

Forty kilometers north of Budapest lays this city with a palace and fortress complex unrivaled by any city in Europe. It's location atop high, rocky hills overlooking the Danube, made it ideal for protecting the territory - and now for a beautiful overlook and green getaway from Budapest.

There is truly something for everyone: hiking, and more extreme sports; museums, historical exhibits and shows; gardens, and breathtaking views of the Danube and some of the highest hills in Hungary. It's the ideal green getaway from Budapest.

Godollo

This summer palace is located about thirty kilometres away from Budapest. Built as a summer residence for the beloved Queen Sisi, it's the massive grounds, beautifully landscaped gardens, and tree lined paths that make it a destination for nature lovers and history buffs alike.

Take the M2 to Ors Vezer Ter Metro Stop and get a ticket at the aboveground green ticket window. Take the HEV to the last stop, Godollo. It's a short walk to the residence and gardens. Entrance to the grounds is free. A tour costs a few euros; there's an excellent cafe inside.

Chapter 16: Viszontlátásra (Goodbye) From Budapest

Budapest is really becoming more and more popular amongst tourists and also expats. Walking down the streets of Budapest you hear a multitude of languages and it's making our beautiful town into quite a cosmopolitan metropolis. If you are reading about Budapest because you're thinking about moving here, you should know you're not the only one. There is quite a big expat community that was drawn at first by the low costs of living and stayed for the diverse cultural experience and the growing economy.

However, don't think everybody will speak English with you and you will be able to get by just like that - while is true in the downtown area is frequented by tourists, once you head deeper into the city you will find a resistance of speaking any other language than Hungarian, mainly because Hungarians are a patriotic people, proud of their culture and language. Learning a little bit of Hungarian will go a long way even as a tourist. You'll make some people happy to see that you are making an effort and you'll get preferential treatment as a guest in our country.

Now, about those low costs of living - that is partly true. Once you start earning local salaries, the quality of living will definitely depend on your salary. The median income lies somewhere around 500 Euros, which can be spent entirely on the price for a 1-bedroom apartment in the central area.

Budapest is so full of charm that it might just make you extend your stay from a few days of visiting to a few years of living. It happens more often than you think and it is a frequent answer when you ask an expat how they ended up living here.

There is so much going on in Budapest and it's still relatively unexplored as it is fairly new to the tourism game, since communism only came down a mere 25 years ago. When travelling to a place like Paris or London you always get a sort of opposition from the locals, as they have grown tired of masses of tourists cramping on their style. In Budapest, locals tend to still be welcoming and friendly to travelers and tourism has done the city plenty of good.

So to wrap it up, one has numerous reasons to choose Budapest as the next destination, be it short term or long term. You have plenty of options when it comes to leisure and entertainment, like the unique thermal baths that are open year round, and you can actually call swimming a hobby and not a summer thing.

Next is the architecture to fall in love with: Art Nouveau, Neo Classical, and Renaissance, mixed in with a bustling nightlife for all tastes. Culture is aplenty with classical music concerts, modern festivals, opera, theatre, cinema (both art house and mainstream), mouth-watering cuisine, and an effervescent restaurant scene. Oh, and the wine. There is so much wine that you can get free tastings on occasions. And if you are not a big wine fan and you prefer the hard stuff, there's pálinka if you can handle it.

PS: Can I Ask You For A Special Favor?

I really hope this book helps you out with your traveling to Budapest!

We would like to ask you for a favour. Would you be kind enough to leave a review for this book on Amazon? It'd be greatly appreciated!

Thanks a lot.

Preview of "Croatia - By Locals"

We edit and publish travel guides from several cities around the world, all written by locals. When planning your next destination, please, check on Amazon to see if we may have covered that city already. If not, we will probably be writing about it soon. Please give us some time.

We would like to give you an advanced look at our Croatia Guide, which is very special. Please take a look:

Chapter 1: Preface - Four Seasons

Croatia is a special little county. On a territory of only 56 542 square kilometers and 31 067 square kilometers of territorial waters it houses a huge diversity of destinations and offers a great selection of stuff worth seeing and doing. Located at the crossroads of Central Europe, Southeast Europe, and the Mediterranean the country goes through 4 seasons and every season has something to offer.

More than a thousand islands in the Adriatic sea and a beautiful coastline for summer, wine cellars and vineyards in autumn scattered all over the country, ski resorts in the mountains for winter and amazing national parks waking up in spring. One of the greatest things about Croatia is that it's not overpopulated and industrialized. There are still intact beaches, nature in its original form all over the country and to top it off there is quite a lot of historical sites around here.

The geographical position and rich history of Croatia has allowed diversity to flourish. Zagreb, the capital of Croatia, is only 400 kilometers away from Split, the second biggest city located in Dalmatia, yet the difference in architecture, cuisine and even mentality is huge. Thanks to its size you can easily rent a car and simply drive around the county and explore all the regions. Compared to other world destinations, Croatia is still pretty affordable. Also, it has good connections to European roads and air traffic. If you're planning a Europe round trip, Croatia is the perfect stop.

Chapter 2: History Of Croatia

The beauty and diversity present today is a direct result of the grand history of this little county. The area known as Croatia today was inhabited throughout the prehistoric period. Remnants of Paleolithic, Neolithic and Chalcolithic cultures have been found all over the country. The most famous site of Neanderthals dating to the middle Paleolithic period is displayed today in Krapina.

The area was also populated during the Greek and Roman rule. Liburnians and Illyrians settled the region, while the first Greek colonies in 6 AD were established on the islands of Korčula, Hvar and Vis. In 9 AD Croatia became part of the Roman Empire. Because of the unique geographical position Croatia was an important part of the Roman Empire.

Diocletian's Palace in Split is one of the most important remains of the Romans while the Pula Arena, still standing today, was one of the biggest amphitheaters of the Roman Empire.

The first ruler to use the Croatian name was duke Trpimir I. in 852. Pope John VIII blessed him, his people and his country making Croatia an official principality. A stone fragment from Šopot, near Benkovac mentions the duke of the Croats, and that's the oldest inscription mentioning the Croatian name.

After the rule of the Croatian dukes, the first king of Croatia was Tomislav in 925 from the Trpimirović dynasty (a dynasty started by duke Trpimir), elevating Croatia to the status of a kingdom. The medieval Croatian kingdom reached its peak in the 11th century during the reigns of Petar Krešimir IV (1058–1074) and Dmitar Zvonimir (1075–1089). From that era the first and most famous document written in Croatian and in a Glagolitic alphabet is Bašćanska ploča, still displayed today in the Croatian Academy of Sciences and Arts.

When Stjepan II died in 1091 ending the Trpimirović dynasty, Ladislaus I of Hungary claimed Croatian crown. Opposition to the claim led to a war and a personal union of Croatia and Hungary in 1102, ruled by Coloman from Árpád dynasty. From that day until 1918 Croatia was bound to Hungary by a personal union. The most important document from that era is the Vinodol statute from 1288. It's the oldest law codex written in Croatian.

For the next four centuries, the Kingdom of Croatia was ruled by the Sabor (parliament) and a Ban (viceroy) appointed by the king. The period saw increasing threat of Ottoman conquest and struggle against the Republic of Venice for control of coastal areas. The Venetians gained control over most of Dalmatia by 1428, with exception of the city-state of Dubrovnik (today's crown jewel of Croatia) which became independent. Ottoman conquests led to the

1493 Battle of Krbava field and 1526 Battle of Mohács, both ending in decisive Ottoman victories. King Louis II died at Mohács, and in 1527 the Croatian Parliament met in Cetin and chose Ferdinand I of the House of Habsburg as new ruler of Croatia. This period saw the rise of influential nobility such as the Frankopan and Zrinski families to prominence and ultimately numerous Bans from the two families.

Following the decisive Ottoman victories, Croatia was split into civilian and military territories, with the partition formed in 1538. The military territories would become known as the Croatian Military Frontier and were under direct Imperial control. Ottoman advances in the Croatian territory continued until the 1593 Battle of Sisak, the first decisive Ottoman defeat, and stabilization of borders.

During the Great Turkish War (1667–1698) Slavonia was regained but western Bosnia, which had been part of Croatia before the Ottoman conquest, remained outside Croatian control. The present-day border between the two countries is a remnant of this outcome. Dalmatia, the southern part of the border, was similarly defined by the Fifth and the Seventh Ottoman–Venetian Wars.

The Ottoman wars instigated great demographic changes. Croats migrated towards Austria and the present-day Burgenland Croats are direct descendants of these settlers. To replace the fleeing population, the Habsburgs encouraged the Christian populations of Bosnia and Serbia to provide military service in the Croatian Military Frontier.

Between 1797 and 1809 the First French Empire gradually occupied the entire eastern Adriatic coastline and a substantial part of its hinterland, ending the Venetian and the Ragusan republics and establishing the Illyrian Provinces. In response the Royal Navy started the blockade of the Adriatic Sea leading to the Battle of Vis in 1811. The Illyrian Provinces were captured by the Austrians in 1813, and absorbed by the Austrian Empire following the

Congress of Vienna in 1815. This led to formation of the Kingdom of Dalmatia and restoration of the Croatian Littoral to the Kingdom of Croatia, now both under the same crown.

The 1830s and 1840s saw romantic nationalism inspire the Croatian National Revival, a political and cultural campaign advocating the unity of all South Slavs in the empire. Its primary focus was the establishment of a standard language as a counterweight to Hungarian, along with the promotion of Croatian literature and culture. During the Hungarian Revolution of 1848 Croatia sided with the Austrians, Ban Josip Jelačić helping defeat the Hungarian forces in 1849, and ushering a period of Germanization policy. The most famous square in Zagreb today holds a statue and is named after Ban Josip Jelačić.

By the 1860s, failure of the policy became apparent, leading to the Austro-Hungarian Compromise of 1867 and creation of a personal union between the crowns of the Austrian Empire and the Kingdom of Hungary.

The treaty left the issue of Croatia's status to Hungary, and the status was resolved by the Croatian–Hungarian Settlement of 1868, when kingdoms of Croatia and Slavonia were united. The Kingdom of Dalmatia remained under Austrian control, while Rijeka retained the status of Corpus separatum introduced in 1779.

After Austria-Hungary occupied Bosnia and Herzegovina following the 1878 Treaty of Berlin, the Croatian Military Frontier was abolished and the territory returned to Croatia in 1881, pursuant to provisions of the Croatian-Hungarian settlement. Renewed efforts to reform Austria-Hungary, entailing federalization with Croatia as a federal unit, were stopped by advent of World War I.

On 29 October 1918 the Croatian Sabor declared independence and decided to join the newly formed State of Slovenes, Croats and Serbs, which in turn entered into union with the Kingdom of Serbia in December 1918 to form the Kingdom of Serbs, Croats, and Slovenes. The 1921 constitution defining the country as a unitary state and abolition of historical administrative divisions effectively ended Croatian autonomy. The new constitution was opposed by the most widely supported national political party—the Croatian Peasant Party (HSS) led by Stjepan Radić.

The political situation deteriorated further as Radić was assassinated in the National Assembly in 1928, leading to the dictatorship of King Alexander of Serbia in January 1929. The dictatorship formally ended in 1931 when the king imposed a more unitarian constitution, and changed the name of the country to Yugoslavia. The HSS, now led by Vladko Maček, continued to advocate federalization of Yugoslavia, resulting in the Cvetković–Maček Agreement of August 1939 and the autonomous Banovina of Croatia.

In April 1941, Yugoslavia was occupied by Germany and Italy. Following the invasion the territory, parts of Croatia, Bosnia and Herzegovina, and the region of Syrmia were incorporated into the Independent State of Croatia (NDH). Parts of Dalmatia were annexed by Italy and the northern Croatian regions of Baranja and Međimurje were annexed by Hungary. The NDH regime was led by Ante Pavelić and ultranationalist Ustaše. The regime introduced anti-semitic laws and conducted a campaign of ethnic cleansing and genocide against Serb and Roma.

A resistance movement soon emerged. On 22 June 1941, the 1st Sisak Partisan Detachment was formed near Sisak, as the first military unit formed by a resistance movement in occupied Europe. This sparked the beginning of the Yugoslav Partisan movement, a communist multi-ethnic anti-fascist resistance group led by Josip Broz Tito. The movement grew rapidly and at the Tehran Conference in December 1943 the Partisans gained recognition from the Allies.

With Allied support in logistics, equipment, training and air power, and with the assistance of Soviet troops taking part in the 1944 Belgrade Offensive, the

Partisans gained control of Yugoslavia and the border regions of Italy and Austria by May 1945.

After World War II, Croatia became a single-party Socialist federal unit of the SFR Yugoslavia, ruled by the Communists, but enjoying a degree of autonomy within the federation. In 1967, Croatian authors and linguists published a Declaration on the Status and Name of the Croatian Standard Language demanding greater autonomy for Croatian language. The declaration contributed to a national movement seeking greater civil rights and decentralization of the Yugoslav economy, culminating in the Croatian Spring of 1971, suppressed by Yugoslav leadership. Still, the 1974 Yugoslav Constitution gave increased autonomy to federal units, basically fulfilling a goal of the Croatian Spring, and providing a legal basis for independence of the federative constituents.

In the 1980s the political situation in Yugoslavia deteriorated with national tension fanned by the 1986 Serbian SANU Memorandum and the 1989 coups in

Vojvodina, Kosovo and Montenegro. In January 1990, the Communist Party fragmented along national lines, with the Croatian faction demanding a looser federation. In the same year, the first multi-party elections were held in Croatia, with Franjo Tuđman's (Croatia's first president) win raising nationalist tensions further. Serbs in Croatia left Sabor and declared the autonomy of areas that would soon become the unrecognized Republic of Serbian Krajina, intent on achieving independence from Croatia.

As tensions rose, Croatia declared independence in June 1991; however the declaration came into effect on 8 October 1991. In the meantime, tensions escalated into the Croatian War of Independence when the Yugoslav National Army and various Serb paramilitaries attacked Croatia. By the end of 1991, a high intensity war fought along a wide front reduced Croatia to control of about two-thirds of its territory. On 15 January 1992, Croatia gained diplomatic recognition by the European Economic Community members, and subsequently the United Nations. The war effectively ended in 1995 with a decisive victory by Croatia in August 1995. The remaining occupied areas were restored to Croatia pursuant to the Erdut Agreement of November 1995, with the process concluded in January 1998. Croatia became a World Trade Organization (WTO) member in 2000. The country signed a Stabilization and Association Agreement (SAA) with the European Union in October 2001. Croatia became member of NATO in 2009, and joined the European Union in July 2013.

Sadly, so many wars, especially the Independence War, left scars all over the country and in the minds and hearts of Croats. Although years passed, the wounds are still not healed, but the county and its people are making progress, rebuilding the destroyed cities and the collective psyche.

The information provided herein is stated to be truthful and consistent, in that any liability, in terms of inattention or otherwise, by any usage or abuse of any policies, processes, or directions contained within is the solitary and utter responsibility of the recipient reader. Under no circumstances will any legal responsibility or blame be held against the publisher for any reparation, damages, or monetary loss due to the information herein, either directly or indirectly.

Respective authors own all copyrights not held by the publisher.

The information herein is offered for informational purposes solely, and is universal as so. The presentation of the information is without contract or any type of guarantee assurance.

The trademarks that are used are without any consent, and the publication of the trademark is without permission or backing by the trademark owner. All trademarks and brands within this book are for clarifying purposes only and are the owned by the owners themselves, not affiliated with this document.

Printed in Great Britain
by Amazon

82803914R00102